The Quirks of Digital Culture

The Quirks of Digital Culture

DAVID BEER
University of York, UK

United Kingdom – North America – Japan – India
Malaysia – China

Emerald Publishing Limited
Howard House, Wagon Lane, Bingley BD16 1WA, UK

First edition 2019

British Library Cataloguing in Publication Data
A catalogue record for this book is available from the British
Library

ISBN: 978-1-78769-916-8 (Paperback)
ISBN: 978-1-78769-913-7 (Online)
ISBN: 978-1-78769-915-1 (Epub)

ISOQAR certified
Management System,
awarded to Emerald
for adherence to
Environmental
standard
ISO 14001:2004.

Certificate Number 1985
ISO 14001

INVESTOR IN PEOPLE

FOR ERIK

CONTENTS

ABOUT THE AUTHOR

David Beer is Professor of Sociology at the University of York. He is the author of *Georg Simmel's Concluding Thoughts* (2019), *The Data Gaze* (2018), *Metric Power* (2016), *Punk Sociology* (2014), *Popular Culture and New Media: The Politics of Circulation* (2013) and *New Media: The Key Concepts* (2008, with Nicholas Gane) and is the Editor of *The Social Power of Algorithms* (2018).

ACKNOWLEDGEMENTS

Thanks go to Emerald and to my editor Jen McCall. Jen's enthusiasm for this project was vital and helped me to build upon my initial sketches. This book is built out of a number of ideas that I have tested out in various blogs and websites over the last three or four years, it includes adaptations and expansions of short pieces published in *Open Democracy*, *The Independent*, *Berfrois*, *Discover Society*, *Louder Than War*, *Sociological Imagination*, and *The Conversation*, as well as pieces I have posted on *Medium*. I have used those pieces a little like music demo tracks. Those short pieces were used to try things out and to experiment with ideas and ways of writing. The book combines, extends and develops those snippets and ideas to bring out the themes and issues. I have worked them together into chapters, extending and appending the points and adding new writing. I would like to thank the various publications and editors for allowing me to explore these thoughts in their publications. Finally, I would like to give extra special thanks to Erik and Martha. When I had the initial idea for this book, which I had whilst listening to a collection of B-sides by the band Jesus and Mary Chain, Erik told me to just do it and not to worry about it, so I have.

personalised experience of reading!

1

DIGITAL CULTURE AND ITS QUIRKS

Last year I began to put a lecture together on memes. I was searching through pages and pages of memes, trying to familiarise myself with what was going on. It was like standing at the edge of a huddle of people who were all laughing together at an inside joke. Some of the memes made sense, lots were unpalatable or offensive, but many more passed me by. And these were just the 'normie' memes, those considered most mainstream and uncool, I didn't even manage to locate the inner circle that is defined by the 'dank' meme. What these pages of memes visualised for me was the deep complexity and unfathomability of this scene. I was confronted with an insider/outsider terminology and images, trends that arrive and die-out quickly, heightened ephemerality and the piling-up of cultural detritus on a mass scale. It was not just my age that put me on the edge of all of this, the fragmentation and scale of these formations are baffling in itself.

There is something intangible and hard to grasp about culture today. The sheer scale of the mediated world that we are exposed to often seems unfathomable. Its glossy surfaces distract from its shadowy, splintered interior. The dazzling glint makes it hard to see its workings. The big tech companies encourage us to be ever more connected, as if that is the solution to all problems. The more connected we are, they say, the greater the possibilities and the purer the social experience. Based on some powerful promises, in the last 10 years a dizzying range of devices and media platforms have worked their way into our lives, shifting how we live, what we know, what we encounter and how we connect with each other. 'Platform Capitalism',[1] as it has been called, may be burgeoning, but we also have something close

PLATFORM CAPITALISM

1

[handwritten marginalia: "living within on & within 2", "New politics of visibility", "ON", "!!!", "REDUCTION", "INTERPE-LLATION", "to interrupt / speak"]

to a new type of *on-demand* or *platform* culture emerging. As we live on and *within* platforms, so culture takes on and becomes mediated by their properties. There are some noticeable and profound changes to culture that are occurring with these moves. As a result, algorithms order that world for us, curating it, giving us the bits that they, according to their coding models, think that we are most likely to react to. We end up with a reductive and smoothed-out version of the deafening noise of content that is out there. A whole new politics of visibility is emerging, in which power is in the hands of those who manage to get heard over the rumbling noise of all that content. This type of glossy visibility is embodied in various ways, from social media influencers and famous YouTubers, to celebrities' social media profiles through to algorithmically defined news feeds and recommendations. The volume of content out there is chaotic and messy, a massive cultural din, a cacophony of voices, ideas and views.

Writing in April 1970 the Marxist thinker Louis Althusser offered a series of reflections on the reproduction of capitalism. The resulting essay 'Ideology and the Ideological State Apparatus'[2] attempted to understand how ideas and beliefs could circulate in ways that enable the structures, hierarchies and labour practices of capitalism to continue. We need not buy into all of the arguments in that essay to see value in one of the key concepts that it offers, 'interpellation'. In one famous passage Althusser claims that '*all ideology hails or interpellates concrete individuals as concrete subjects*'.[3] His argument continues by suggesting that we become subjects when exposed to the ideologies woven into culture. As such, these ideologies 'recruit' us as subjects. Althusser continues by building towards some distinctive imagery:

> ideology 'acts' or 'functions' in such a way that it 'recruits' subjects among the individuals (it recruits them all), or 'transforms' the individual into subjects (it transforms them all) by that very precise operation which I have called interpellation or hailing, and which can be imagined along the lines of the most commonplace everyday police (or other) hailing: 'Hey, you there!'[4]

The concept of interpellation is about attention, inescapability and the way in which ideology finds us. This combination of features is captured in Althusser's claim that: 'assuming that the theoretical scene I have imagined takes place in the street, the hailed individual will turn round'.[5] As we spin

to hail, attract attention

to face the voice, we are interpellated. The point here is that we can't help but turn towards the hailing voice and in so doing we are exposed to those ideologies embedded in culture. We become interpellated in our reflex response to hearing those calls. This doesn't just pose questions about the drawing of our attention, it also requires reflection on which hailing we respond to, how we react and how we become subjected to wider ideas about the world. There is, Althusser goes on to claim, no outside to ideology and we can't resist the hailing. Althusser even suggests that we can be made to feel that we are somehow outside or removed from how ideology works and how it acts on us, but this is to mislead ourselves.[6] It is this moment of the subjection of individuals to culture that we could question further. We might wonder how interpellation works in today's fragmented and complex mediated landscape.

moment of subjection

The masses of content crammed into and piling up on these platforms constantly shouts for our attention. Louis Althusser's vision of 'interpellation' needs to be rethought a little. The shouts of 'hey you there!'[7] come from many more sources. We still can't help but turn to face the caller, but where to look first and how long should that thing sustain our attention? Now that street-scene that Althusser used as a metaphor is crammed full of people desperately screaming our monikers, repeatedly. It leaves us spinning. We still can't help but look, we are still interpellated, but we are never quite sure which call to respond to or which way to look. The call is inescapable but has become much more disorientating as we spin to the various sources of that haling. All these agendas compete for our attention, influencing the systems and the content that shape our everyday lives. There is an inescapable maelstrom of 'pulsating life'[8] that we are expected to interface with and contribute to. That might seem a daunting prospect when put it like that, yet we have become fairly accustomed to navigating these scenes, it is so familiar to us that we have become highly skilled at managing these environments, even if we can't always cope with them.

nickname 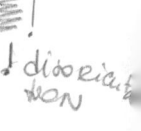 *disorientation*

The on-demand nature of cultural consumption has also changed the *rhythms* and *gaps* of entertainment and distraction: from stories of the use of our data, the 'flickering friendships'[9] of social media and fast moving memes, through to the disruption of traditional media outlets and on to the way we are connected, networked and interfaced. It is hard to know where to start if we want to understand what is happening. As the hailing becomes multidirectional, so the ideologies people grab onto to can become more fragmented. The shifts in culture that we are seeing are outpacing our understanding of them. Algorithms are layered one-on-one, shaping decision-making processes and meshing together different forms of agency. Our phones have moved from momentary tools of connection to being deeply embedded in our everyday and bodily practices. Let me just pause here to check my notifications … again. Social media haven't just added a new means for maintaining our relationships, they have altered how we live and how we understand those relations. It is worth noting here that Facebook, with a typically virtuous claim about focussing on 'meaningful relationships', plan to add a dating service to their platform to rival Tinder.[10] Couched in this normalising language and despite the concerns over data use it seems that they seek to create greater data intimacy and to intervene ever further into social relations.

Research has also suggested that data are extracted in many different ways by the apps we have running on our smartphones. It is not only the companies operating those apps accessing our data but much of it also ends up circulating into the hands of a small number of tech giants – with 88% of the app harvested data ending up in the hands of Alphabet and over 40% of it in the hands of Facebook.[11] This is without even considering the archetypal platform WeChat, that incorporates everything from purchasing to messaging, and which users never need to leave. There is a complexity and scale to data extraction and use, of which most is beyond our awareness. A recent report from Doteveryone has indicated the limited knowledge that people have over their data use, which is complemented by the sense of a lack of control that they feel they have over those data.[12] For instance, that report indicated that 80% of people weren't aware that 'information which other people share about them is collected', culture is unfathomable and so is the data infrastructure through which it is consumed. What we might think of as privacy – and the perception of privacy – has altered as we turn our lives into media content and as the large tech companies and other actors seek to gain insights into how we live, what we do and who we are. If I were writing this paragraph 10 years ago it would have sounded hyperbolic, but now I am probably understating the case. Digital or on-demand culture is not just about what we demand; it also demands things of us. It demands our attention, it demands our activity, it demands our engagement, it demands our lives, our tastes, our choices and our data.

Amongst all this chaos it is hard to understand what is unfolding. The breadth of these fluxes is baffling, ranging from the trivial to the apparently momentous. On the surface it is often the case that the features of our digital culture don't seem to represent much beyond a fleeting moment, a surface effect, some brief flickering event or an attention-grabbing bit of gossip. It would be easy to dismiss such things as glossy, superficial and ephemeral. In many ways they are, yet this doesn't mean that they don't represent something more substantial. It would be easy to ignore a lot of the here-today-gone-tomorrow bits of culture that we routinely encounter and to which we give a little thought. Some of these ephemera, these fleeting things, actually call for us to pause and take seriously what they mean, even if they themselves are quite disposable or appear inconsequential. Those *quirks* matter; they can be used to reveal something; they give us a way into exploring the particular dynamics of the culture and media that shape our lives – affording us ways into seeing the powerful inequalities, prejudices, maltreatments and divisions that are at play along with the new connections, changes and shifts. Digital culture can seem decorative, yet it is still defined by ruptures as much as by the new connections it enables.

As digital culture has been lifted on to media platforms, our everyday experiences are full of quirks. Often unnoticed, these quirks accumulate and occupy our daily experiences. It is possible that they can be the means by which we come, in aggregate, to know the world and to have a sense of our place within it. This book deals with just a few of those quirks. The volume of experiences in the splintering mediascape mean that I am only scratching the surface with my selections, I am only touching upon the underpinning patterns and dynamics. Plus, I am, of course, only responding to things that come into my orbit, which is also inevitably a product of these media circulations themselves. This book seeks to ask questions about what is going on and to find openings, it is by no means definitive or complete. Indeed, we might wonder if a complete vision is possible given the maelstrom of culture and media today. The chapters that follow focus upon these little tangles and creases to explore the often strange but compelling processes that they reveal or encapsulate. Each quirk is a kind of microcosm of the state of things, each can be used to create a small tear through which we might see how our lives are being shaped by these cultural formations.

This book deals with a series of such quirks. It opens them up, examines them and reflects on what their presence reveals. It looks at the fragments of our fragmentary experiences, what the classical sociologist Georg Simmel once described as 'the fragmentary character of life',[13] to see what each shard might say. I hope that you will see each of the chapters as containing a series of provocations or brief reflections on these rapid and swirling media spaces that we occupy – from old episodes of TV game shows, to the end of phone directories, through to the connections we have with our devices and the personalisation of advertising. Each chapter is an opening, a pause for reflection in this gusting cultural landscape. The chapters don't fit together to create a complete jigsaw. Instead the book reflects something of what it is like to live in the fragments of a platform or on-demand culture. Looking at the fragments, pausing on the quirks, can give us little glimpses behind the curtain and a sense of what is driving and shaping the highly mediated lives we lead.

This book is presented like a vinyl record, a mini-album or EP perhaps, you can drop the stylus wherever you like. There are no prerequisites, the reader can drop in and out, or you can choose listen all the way through. Each of the chapters unpicks a series of quirks to reveal something more at play. It couldn't possibly cover all of the events and issues that have arisen over recent years, one of the points is that these fragments are too numerous to be seen all at once. Instead it is selective, buzzing towards things that begin to build a picture. In this sense, what I offer here is inspired by what David Frisby once described as 'sociological impressionism'.[14] The quirks gathered in its pages are intended to give an impression of the shifts that are now shaping our lives. The importance of *the quirk* is that it gives a little rupture that we can use, in broad brush strokes, to sketch out that impression.

Of course, what I am describing here as platform or on-demand culture – by which we can mean culture produced for and consumed through the many available platforms, from Netflix to Spotify, Facebook to Amazon, Youtube, Google, Instagram, Twitter, WeChat, Deliveroo and the like through to gaming platforms like Roblox or Minecraft – is inseparable from the dynamics of the new types of capitalism that are emerging. In its simplest form this is a kind of capitalism that is almost entirely underpinned by data. Yet this is not the only change. Power is now working in some novel and interesting ways, acting upon us in frequently unseen and unnoticed ways. This is partly about the use of our data, but it goes further.

anti-elite elite (handwritten)

A BIT MORE CONTEXT: CREW-NECK CAPITALISM

crew-neck !!! (handwritten)

Capitalism has long been defined by collars. Blue or white: collars have crudely demarcated belonging, status and position. A different collar is now taking on a defining role in contemporary capitalism: the crew neck. Like the collars that went before, this collar symbolises an underlying agenda and logic.

The major players in what has been referred to by Nick Srnicek as 'platform capitalism'[15] embody crew-neck capitalism and its values. They eschew the collar and tie combination in favour of crew-neck comfort. This projects a certain image, of a non-hierarchical, non-commercial and carefree status. An apparent anti-elite elite is created that has positioned itself in a way that seems to render it immune to the anti-elite sentiment – it even draws its status from it. It aligns itself with such anti-elitism and so avoids becoming its target. It is not just that the capitalist's attire has become more casual, it is that capitalism has taken on an appearance of casualness in order to distract from its behaviours, actions and authorities. *(Ro's coolness)* (handwritten)

techno Jan ↓ 2012 ↓ 2019 (handwritten)

DISTRACT. (handwritten)

Crew-neck capitalism is about casualisation. Casualisation on all fronts. A casual adornment is symbolic of the casualisation of the relations of production and consumption. The nature of work and the nature of consumer interaction are embodied in the crew neck. Crew-neck capitalism promotes the idea that all labour, like its fashions, should be as casual as possible – hence the crew neck reflects and somehow justifies the now familiar problems of casualised labour. The hyper-insecurity of the gig economy is the archetypal model here. The crew neck says that all work should be casual in style and causal in form. This casualisation of clothing is a veil for the collateral casualties of this form of capitalism. Alongside this, the style of the crew-neck capitalist lulls the consumer towards a sense of comfortable acceptance and reassured engagement with their products.

CASUALISATION (handwritten)

The crew neck itself is symbolic, it tells you not to worry, it says that they are one of you not one of them. Rather than being some distant moneymaker, the crew-neck capitalist likes you to think that they share your outlook and values. The attire erodes the sense of distance and veils power. It is more than a clothing choice by these powerful individuals, it captures and projects certain properties. A casualness of demeanour could well distract from what Zygmunt Bauman once referred to as the 'collateral damage' of capitalism.[16]

So that they appear as friends in your dreams (handwritten)

The crew-neck capitalist can make off-the-cuff comments about protecting the integrity of national elections and no one will recoil in horror. Indeed, it can be seen as helpful of them to make such promises. They seek to be trusted with this bizarre and worrying level of power that they wield. They want you to feel ok about it.

A crew-neck capitalist is fairly easy to spot. They usually run a large tech company – or they might be found in prototype form in smaller start-ups or in those interloper companies that get bought up by the tech giants. The exit strategy is a valued asset of the nascent crew necker.

Most common with some of the biggest tech firms, this is a mode of presentation replicated increasingly in other types of companies. It calls out: I don't need to dress for the job I have, because status doesn't matter, I built it and now I just happen to run this thing.

But it is not just the clothing that matters, rather the clothing is representative of an approach, an image and a set of ideals. The casual tone and familiarity permeates down into our interactions with these companies and platforms. This tone is peppered across the interactions and points of contact that we have with crew-neck capitalism (some of which I will highlight in later chapters). It is highly likely that we have all experienced the causal tone and over familiarity of an app or software update message, or we have received messages of Christmas or birthday wishes from a company that doesn't know us, or we have faced the constant encouragement to tell them, our capitalists friends, what is going on in our lives. It is a learned unprofessional tone that eases us into a sense that no one around here is anything like a hard-nosed capitalist, no one, we are reassured, is in any way trying to exploit us. They just want us all to connect together to make a better world. They project the friendly facilitator type image, playing down the money, power and influence.

The casualness brings a kind of distancing from older more formal approaches, the new tech is not managed in those old ways, so they tell us. The tech leaders no longer see themselves as distant from their customers. Instead, the casualness in the clothing and tone is part of an attempt at giving an impression of a break down in hierarchy. They are no longer dominating us or managing the production of value from our custom, instead they are like us and they have the enhancement of our experiences in mind. At least that seems to be the message. Everything is about the user experience and how that can be enhanced, even where the notion of experience *tailored pure desired experience*

9

is itself used as a way to render acceptable the use of our data and the targeting of our lives.

The crew-neck capitalist seeks to sell ideals; these are ideals or visions of a kind of pure or perfect experience that can be pursued in perpetuity. This future, which they assume we also want, stands as a kind of imagined perfect experience in which we are never disrupted, in which our social spaces are ever more tailored to us, where we encounter the things that suit us or that reinforce our identities. This pure experience that they promote as being our shared destination is, they imagine, free from malevolence and subversion, it is exactly, they suggest, as we would want it to be. A perfect and perfectible social environment where all they are prioritising is our *very narcissistic* experience. That is the vision of the crew-neck capitalist. They make out that our experience is central to everything and that serving that experience is their calling; the rest, it would seem, falls into place in response to that calling. Their mission, far from being economically driven, is simply to remove the impurities from those experiences and to make them increasingly pure. The notion of *experience* becomes a powerful part of the rhetoric of the crew-neck capitalist, it is the thing they fall back on to justify and legitimate their every action.

Overall, their T-shirts tell us not to worry for they are one of us rather than being one of those other exploitative capitalists. It is important not to be distracted by their casual attire or their informal tone, these techno-capitalists mean business. And their business is to turn our lives into economic value. This model of capitalism requires a casual faux-familiarity because it is reliant on us sharing things with it and engaging with it on its own terms. These media demand intimacy, and so they need a familiar feel.

We find the casual tone of the crew-neck capitalist all around us in the platforms of our digital culture, we hardly even notice its presence, it has already become too familiar. We are often addressed in a kind of ironic or playful tone, a tone intended to make us feel at ease, like we can trust the platform and like they are one of us, providing the things we want, sharing our values and having our best possible experiences as their goal. They often assume that we share their ideals or their visions of a desirable future. When we hear casual discussions of purer experiences, perfect convenience or growing connections, the question we could ask the crew-neck capitalist is what they are using that pursuit of a pure experience to achieve. It may well be used to justify some attempts to extract more data or to make some form of surveillance and targeting seem like it is in our best interest.

This is the capitalist underpinnings of our cultural scene. The book feeds out from these initial observations, thinking about the way that those forms of power seep into everyday life in different forms whilst also considering how the features of our digital or platform culture open up what is happening within capitalism in some revealing ways. The language of convenience, experience and opportunity are part of this. If we want to understand how life is transforming, we need to understand what happens when culture moves onto platforms. Some of the biggest questions we face today – about how politics works, about how we connect with each other, about how we are nudged or our behaviours are guided, about how discretion might be eroded or social relations unhinged, about how we might withdraw or how we might get tangled into intense interaction, how worlds and worldviews are shaped, and so on – are connected with the types of platform-based culture that we now participate within. Culture has changed in the last decade or so, the platform defined cultures that have emerged are not as inconsequential or superficial as they might seem, they are all about power, politics and the remaking of what we might still want to call the social world that we occupy. This book is not an attack on these platforms, I am not whining about some lost halcyon or analogue days, it is an attempt to acknowledge and understand something that will continue to have a profound influence over our lives long into the future. How we then choose to live within platform culture can at least be something we have an active part within.

* FANTASTICALLY ACCURATE USE OF ADJ-s
(UNUSUAL ENG + ACAD WRITING)

* ♂♂♀

* the rationale of the (IN-)VISIBLE
(new meaning)

* MATERIALITY of digit culture
CROSS-mech: cult-econ-cult

* POWER in the centre

* critical & clear
* CASUAL FAMILIARITY = vast

2

THE ORDER OF THINGS

At 12.12 p.m. on the 23 May 2018 the tech leader and enthusiast Elon Musk tweeted to propose that a new kind of metric system could be developed that would be used to rate the trustworthiness of particular articles, journalists or publications. This, he thought, would solve the problem of the out-of-control circulation of inaccuracies and misinformation across social media. His excitement about his own idea was typically palpable. His tweet reads:

> *Going to create a site where the public can rate the core truth of any article & track the credibility score over time of each journalist, editor & publication. Thinking of calling it Pravda ....*

Putting aside the lack of any concern for where it is that people might draw the ability to judge core truth, and ignoring that media sources may be the resource against which people make such judgments about truth in the first place, Musk seems to think that the problems of misleading content online might be solved by metrics. The vision here is that articles can be rated and scored for their truthfulness, which then feeds into rankings for those involved in their writing or production. The result is that metrics can be used to lend certain views authority and legitimacy whilst relegating those that are considered untrustworthy into obscurity. Put simply, Musk wishes to create a metric and ranking of trustworthiness. Of course, there are lots of problems here, not least the point that people will review based upon existing worldviews they hold and what they want to read, and so such a system is inevitably doomed to exacerbate rather than resolve its intended purpose. Putting these problems aside for the moment, what this tweet is suggestive of is a trust in data and metrics. As I will explore in this chapter, there is a *new order of things* emerging at the points where data and culture converge – it is imagined that on-demand culture can be organised, shaped and improved through the data it produces. This is one glimpse into the order of things, but how can we get to grips with these logics?

With all the shifts of contemporary culture, we often think about what this means for the individual. But how is the movement of culture onto platforms leading to new structural configurations and facilitating new ways of ordering cultural forms? What is the new order of things within which those individual experiences are shaped? So many competing categories, classifications, labels and rankings now present themselves to us. The complexity and fragmentary nature of these media-dense environments brings inevitable attempts to simplify, reduce and box. The vastness of the content creates the impulse to classify and to impose some order, the alternative would be a cultural scene that is impossible to comprehend. And so genres proliferate, labels, tags and types multiply. The greater the range and volume of content, the more significant and extensive are the means by which that content is organised for us and by us. The result of the speediness and instant nature of digital culture, as well as the scale and depth of cultural content, has brought the ordering process much higher up in the mix. Where culture is consumed on-demand, so comes the playlist, the sub-genre, the search-term, the various and changing categories on the dashboards of Netflix and other providers. These are the new grids in which content is placed, classified and organised. We are constantly faced with a need to classify our own content and to work with the many different systems of classification used by others.[17] New regimes of classification and ordering emerge in such circumstances, especially where organising and self-organising systems combine. From the hashtag to the categorisation of TV shows, a new order of things is emerging in culture. Much more active in its form and far more varied in its labels, this order of things is hard to comprehend but is a familiar part of how we now engage with culture. Rather than providing a lengthy exploration, let us instead start to explore these issues by focussing on the end of three print and paper staples of cultural ordering: the phone book, the music newspaper and the postal cards that used to be included in records and CDs.

RIPPING UP THE *YELLOW PAGES*

The announcement that the *Yellow Pages* was to cease its 50-year print run in January 2019[18] reminded me of the grimacing strongman Geoff Capes. In the 1980s, the ability to rip a phone directory in half seemed to be an ultimate symbol of human strength. In fact, *The Guinness Book of Records* still carries a number of records for phonebook tearing – the greatest number of phonebooks ripped from the spine in one minute is 33.[19] Yet when the last copy of the *Yellow Pages* is delivered, its ongoing legacy will not be limited to such trivia.

Launched in 1966, the *Yellow Pages* is perhaps the best known classified business directory. Known for its bulky presence, hence the wonder at ripping, it became a staple in homes and workplaces. When a business or service was needed, the *Yellow Pages* was a trusted source. The most recent version stretches from abattoirs to yoga, covering everything from taxidermists to graffiti removal. Inevitably the rise of the internet has led to a dwindling interest in these artefacts of a slower age. The comparative slimness of the recent editions is testament to this; the book is getting smaller with each passing year. Ripping the *Yellow Pages* is no longer quite such a feat.

The famous *Yellow Pages* TV adverts give a sense of the importance and cultural reach of these hefty yellow books. Stretching across the 1980s and 1990s, the best known of these adverts involved a man attempting to track down a book. Working his way through the list of booksellers, JR Hartley finally tracked down a rare copy of his own book "Fly Fishing". This was part of a series of adverts in which people turned to the *Yellow Pages* for help – in another case a house party leaves a young man in need of a French polisher to remove a scratch from a table before his parents arrive home from holiday. Yell, who are behind *Yellow Pages*, even have a 'classic adverts' section of these adverts on their YouTube channel.[20] In all cases, these books were depicted as a comforting presence that could impose order, help us to find the things we needed, resolve problems and allow us to negotiate a complex world. The classic adverts stick in the mind partly because of how smart they were, but the apparent power of the *Yellow Pages* to render a messy world knowable and accessible also played a part.

As these adverts suggest, the influence of the *Yellow Pages* is actually to be found in the power of its classifications. A little of that power can be found reflected in company names. Today we have companies preoccupied with search engine optimisation, aimed at getting the highest possible position in Google searches. Something similar happened with the *Yellow Pages*, but instead of the logic of Google's PageRank algorithm[21] governing namings, it was the alphabetised classifications that held sway. As well as choosing what category to be included within and what type of listing to have, companies would sometimes also name themselves with this format in mind. If you looked for a taxi for instance, you would be confronted with a series of attempts to game the format – with A1, AAA and so on, used so as to appear as early as possible within the listing. This is a small indicator of how the classificatory systems we use actually come to shape the world as well as what we know of it.

Classifications don't just shape behaviours, they also influence what we know of the world and what we can discover. In their book *Sorting Things Out*, Geoffrey Bowker and Susan Leigh Star[22] explored the many ways that classifications play a part in how our lives are ordered – from the classification of people, types of work and medicines to the way we organise our homes. They found that we develop our own classificatory systems that contrast and match with the broader classifications that we are given. Think, for instance, of the way that music is organised.[23] We may have our own means for organising our music collections and playlists, and these might compete with broader genre classifications.

In the classic book *The Order of Things*, Michel Foucault provided a historical account of the importance of classifications for shaping how knowledge develops.[24] In that book, Foucault looks at how classificatory systems are established and embedded in the development of knowledge. The message is clear, how we order the world matters. Categories shape what is known and how things are then understood. Take the use of what have been described as 'sensitive interests' in targeted advertising, which have made it possible to target based on sexuality, religion, political beliefs and so on[25] – here the politics of classification is acutely felt and can be used to directly discriminate and to perpetuate prejudice and inequality.

Foucault suggested that the classifications we use form a grid. When we encounter objects, places, people, animals and the like, our 'encoded eye' places them within those grids. The result is that those grids have a big influence on how we see the world around us. Categories and grids can be powerful in helping us to manage a baffling world, they can be liberating.

They also bring limits and can push us towards reductive, restrictive and even damaging interpretations and attitudes. Theodor Porter, in his work on the trust we place in numbers and quantification, has argued that categories can have the effect of 'abstracting away their individuality'.[26] Such categories have the effect, Ian Hacking has suggested, of 'making people up'.[27] It is for this type of reasons that Imogen Tyler has argued that we should be more aware of the 'consequences of classificatory systems and the forms of value, judgments and norms they establish'.[28] In this vein, to pick just one pertinent example, Nisha Kapoor and Kasia Narkowicz's ground breaking work illustrates just how damaging the blunt application of categories like citizenship can be.[29] The point is that categories are not neutral things nor are they natural or fixed, their selection and application is an active presence that frames how we see and approach the world. Of course, the *Yellow Pages* is in no way a damaging presence, but it might give us pause to reflect more broadly on the part that categories play, especially as they are being reshaped by social media and the like.

As an extension of things like classified newspaper advertising, the *Yellow Pages* was a significant part of the development and cementing of the classificatory grid that orders the world for us. As classifications continue to shape knowledge, they will carry traces of things like phone directories, even as we move on to new media forms. They will live on in the way that content is classified in things like Twitter lists, Pinterest boards, Spotify playlists, tagged images on Instagram, Snapchat and Facebook and even in the hashtags we use. These classifications are mutating in new directions as the media themselves change. Classifications in social media are notably more dynamic and varied in their form.

An obvious observation to make about the end of the *Yellow Pages* in print is that it provides yet another marker of the move to an online and immaterial world. However, there is more to understanding what this endpoint might reveal. The *Yellow Pages* was part of the story of how we have come to classify the social world. Its print run might have come to an end, but the impulse to categorise and classify complexity and mess will continue. It is in the way that it provided and cemented classificatory ways of approaching the world that the legacy of the *Yellow Pages* will continue. Underpinning all of this is the dynamism of classification that accompanies the unfathomable volume of cultural content that arises as culture has moved onto tech platforms.

THE END OF THE *NME* AND THE CHANGING SOURCES OF CULTURAL INFORMATION

A little like the *Yellow Pages*, the reasons for the end of the print version of the *NME*, which came to a conclusion in 2018, hardly need stating.[30] Once music news began to accelerate, boosted by the internet and social media, the weekly format was always likely to end up looking ponderous. When it comes to music culture, being behind-the-times is never a good thing. Now is hot, last Thursday isn't. As the cycles of music news tightened, becoming more immediate, the *NME* print edition found itself on the outside. So the story goes.

This looks like the latter stages of a process that started to unfold around 12 years ago. It was in 2006 when *Top of the Pops* lost its weekly TV slot[31] – becoming, instead, the fold-up chair that is pulled out during seasonal festivities. The monuments of music culture were starting to crumble. The same arguments appeared back then. Music, the BBC told us, was being consumed differently and in ways that clashed with a prime-time TV show. In short, these music cultures had raced off in the other direction.

What is amazing is how long the *NME* kept its print operation alive. The death-throws of a move to a free pick-up in 2015 didn't resolve the problem. It was never likely to either. That particular move is now being post-rationalised as an attempt to use the bigger free print distribution to bring new readers to the online format.[32]

There is no doubt that we have moved into a quite different cultural era, signalled by the end of these old familiar sources of music news. In the mid-1990s the media theorist Mark Poster argued that we were moving into a 'second media age'[33] – a more immaterial and connected period dominated by digital media. The reality is far more diverse than such a rupture might suggest. Vinyl and hardback sales have reversed downward trends and the thriving live music and comedy scenes are examples that suggest that there remains an impulse for a more tangible and tactile relationship with the culture we consume.

The pull towards nostalgia is likely to make us reflect on what the final issue of the *NME* means and what has been lost. On hearing the news about the *NME*, I was transported back to a time of buying the paper, as it was then, and sometimes a CD before heading home to revel. I would choose between the *NME* and *Melody Maker* on a cover-by-cover basis – occasionally buying both. The *NME* opened up a world that I couldn't really get anywhere else. The London focus was annoying on occasion, but I would still read it cover-to-cover. The reviews were crucial to choose where my limited money might be spent or to just see what was coming out. The gig listings were a guide to possible or imagined excursions. The interviews and news stories provided glimpses of attitudes, opinions and views that gave the music a different tint. The pictures gave some fashion codes to echo. Music weeklies were almost the exclusive source of such detail.

Instead of being exclusive to music weeklies these things are now everywhere. Far from being lost, they are available in over-abundance. The music weekly made music cultures digestible – they curated it for us and fitted it into the limited pagination. Outside of its previous page and word limits, music news now has few constraints. We have not lost something so much as gained far more than we can manage. The music information available to us today is overwhelming, its fragmentation and eclecticism seem to be reflected in how music is consumed.

The *NME* worked as a weekly when culture was more containable. Where once journalists and particularly editors chose what filtered through to us, the mass of unstructured music information and sounds are now filtered by algorithms – from trending lists and news feeds to automated playlists. The taste-makers have, to varying degrees, become algorithmic.[34] The nostalgic laments that followed the announcement about the print version of the *NME* are more than likely representative of a nostalgia for a cultural landscape that wasn't quite so overwhelming and where those that decided what music we encountered weren't quite so faceless and nameless – that is except, of course, for the enigma that was Johnny Cigarettes. Without the anchor points of broadcast and print, the flow of information and news about culture and cultural events is decentralised and is swept along in the cross-currents of social media exchanges of different sorts. The result is not just a changing set of underlying principles but also a growing sense of the complexity and scale of culture. Where the end of the *Yellow Pages* suggests some changes in the classification of culture, the end of the *NME* indicates a shift towards new types of cultural curation.

WHATEVER HAPPENED TO THE MYSTERIOUS EPICENTRE OF THE BRITISH MUSIC SCENE?

There is one inauspicious address that has a unique presence in British music: 3 Alveston Place, Leamington Spa. It's an address that conjures memories for those who bought music in the pre-streaming era. But what has become of it?

3 Alveston Place, Leamington Spa is an address that is likely to ring a familiar tone. Anybody who bought their music on vinyl, CD or tape is almost certain to have come across this address. These formats usually carried a second-class freepost card that was almost always made out to the same address – with the band or singer's name added at the top. The card invited you to write your details on the reverse before posting. Returning the card registered you for postal updates. The slow speed of this all seems quaint on reflection.

Even infrequent music buyers are likely to have noticed that all of their favourite bands and singers appeared to live in the same house. During the 1990s I had no idea that Leamington Spa was in the Midlands, even though I lived there, making it an ideal spot for distributing materials across the UK. My vision at the time was not so much of a house like that shared by The Monkees, but of something much more industrial: a house with a production line of flyers and pamphlets being placed into envelopes and bagged up for posting. The vision I had was much closer to the Malibu Stacy doll factory on *The Simpsons*. The scale of the task, managing the correspondence for the entire British music scene, seemed like it would be impossible to cope with. I knew the address well, yet I had no idea what went on there or what it looked like.

As I was getting my music information from elsewhere, I didn't feel the need to post many of these cards. I tried a couple of times and I don't think I remember getting very much back. Just some gig flyers and new release pamphlets. Although I do remember sending off to get a special bonus CD insert booklet for a 60ft Dolls album, I got that. I know I didn't send many off because when I go back to my old music I am often confronted with these artefacts of a different musical world. This was a time, as discussed above, in which the materiality and speed of music information was totally different. This transformation is embodied in the small cards that now fall out of the vinyl I buy, no longer do these invite me to have postal correspondence with a small West Midlands town, instead they carry a code for a free download.

After I noticed one of the Alveston Place cards in a 12″ EP version of Embrace's *Fireworks*, I was reminded of this address and thought I would take advantage of the advances of technology to correct the visions I had

had. I searched on Google Street View and could only find a building site. The reason for this then became clear. The original 3 Alveston Place seems to have been demolished.

So what happened to 3 Alveston Place? It's safe to say that it lives on in people's memories. There is quite a bit of nostalgic discussion of the address online. There is even a Twitter account named after it, for instance. It seems that the address was still being used for official music correspondence as late as the 2000s. It was at some point in the first decade of the millennium that the purpose of the building changed, it became a tile shop. According to Warwick District Council's planning records,[35] agreement was then given for the building to be demolished in early 2015. A very short entry in the minutes from the December 2014 meeting reveals that no objections were raised to its demolition.[36] And so its fate was sealed. The historical significance of the building must have been lost somewhere along the line.

3 Alveston place, Leamington Spa, is now a four bedroom, four bathroom new-build town house, with a balcony. It is part of a nine-house Alveston Place development. The Alveston Place website[37] provides details of the house and the sales brochure carries photos of the development.[38] Gleaming new white fronted houses sit in a row. So, the mysterious epicentre of the British music scene is now a town house. No longer needed as the fulcrum of music information, the networks have moved elsewhere affording its rehabilitation as part of the transformation of urban space. The changes at 3 Alveston Place are linked to both the changing flows of music information and changing urban space. I suspect that despite these changes the address will continue to cause a flicker of recognition from those who liked to listen to their music on a material format. This makes me wonder if the new residents will occasionally get a card through the door addressed to an unfamiliar name. Perhaps they will return it to sender, I am sorry, Black Grape don't live here anymore.

Where the end of the *Yellow Pages* and the *NME* indicates shifts in classification and curation, the fate of 3 Alveston Place is a part of the same trends but in this case it highlights the shifting infrastructures of connection and distribution in culture. An early stage in direct marketing and targeting, 3 Alveston place was quickly pushed aside once decentralised media forms facilitated much more direct and rapid points of contact. Why post a card and wait when you can instead get an instant push-notification?

THE CHAOS OF MUSIC GENRES

The types of transitions exemplified in microcosm in the three endpoints I have covered so far in this chapter highlight some new forms of cultural ordering and information flows – notably in classification, curation and the infrastructure of distribution. If we stick for the moment with music, we can get a hint of how this is playing out in the cultures themselves. A few years ago I recall trying to understand a new music genre called seapunk. It stuck in my head. It was a moment when it occurred to me just how much genre had changed. I was baffled. Then again music genre is baffling. It would seem that where we once had relative simplicity, we now have something much more vital and chaotic. So, what was happening with music genre? We might recall the simple pleasure of browsing a local record store and its neatly segregated sections of rock and pop and, if you were in a big enough megastore, classical, jazz and maybe even world music. The systems of classification in these spaces were quite simple. You could visit the chart sections, which were of course organised by the volume of sales during the previous week, or you could explore the rest of the store's content by its alphabetical position. And then you would also have the choice of format: vinyl, tape or CD. As I work on the final parts of this book the final high street music chain HMV has just called in administrators for the second time in six years, it's future looks far from certain.[39]

Informed by friends, radio and the music weeklies, we might then have layered some genre categories on top of this broader layout in order to help us to refine our tastes, these might have included such comfortable labels as indie, punk, soul, house, hip hop and the like. Easy. But things have become more complicated in music cultures, to the extent that they are almost inaccessible to the uninitiated and probably not fully comprehendible even to the most dedicated music fan. It was only on returning to genre for a small research project that I began to see the scale of the complexity that is music genre today.[40]

We are, of course, all quite familiar now with stories about the changes in music consumption that have occurred over the last decade or so – I have outlined some of these in this chapter already. What we have heard less about is what these cultural and technological changes mean for the music itself and for the way that music listeners organise and classify culture. We know quite a bit about the music industry, copyright and the financial impact of downloading and streaming. A lot less attention has been given to the ordering of the music cultures themselves, how they are organised and the meaning attached to this widely available cacophony of sounds. One thing is very clear, it takes a good deal of commitment to keep up with the changes that are taking place, and even more commitment to have any sense of the broader movements that are happening in music.

What is defining the change in music cultures is not just eclecticism, but the actual fragmentation of music cultures themselves. Facilitated by the accessibility of music through streaming services, there is a splintering of music and an escalation of options and opportunities. More music, means a greater need to organise, which means a proliferation of genre. It is not just that people like a variety of types of music but that this variety of music available has proliferated to unprecedented levels. Indeed, there is already an established argument in subcultural and post-subcultural work, much of which was written before streaming, that music cultures are becoming more fragmented and less coherent. This would certainly seem to be the case were we to spend some time trying to get to grips with what is going on in contemporary music. Fragmentation would certainly be the motif. We might speculate that decentralised media, such as those typical of social media, lead to decentralised cultures. Without focal points like Top of the Pops, the music press and the like, music cultures have no fixed anchors – or at least they have fewer centres of gravity holding things back. We might still have charts, but these are now far less relevant, and have been replaced by trending lists, constantly updated playlists and other real-time measures of what is buzzing. So, on one side music cultures are fragmenting and on the other they appear to be speeding up. Music cultures are not tied into the types of structures that dominated the last 50 years or so, instead they are much more mobile, esoteric and ephemeral. They move quickly and in lots of directions. Sometimes these directions are nostalgic and cyclical, other times they are about musical hybrids and in other instances they simply splinter out into new territories, with new combinations of influences, inspired by viral social connections, neologisms and emergent discourses.

We might wonder how we can understand such a set of developments in music cultures or in the cultural shifts that they are a part of. We can't hope to be able to see across all of these small-scale and interlinked developments in music genres. Even those on the inside are unlikely to be able to do this. Music streaming has burst the barriers of consumption, enabling eclecticism and new patterns of consumption. That is to say that amongst the apparent chaos people appear to enjoy certain combinations of genres rather than unconstrained cultural gluttony. The raft of labels on Netflix and YouTube categories suggest something similar is going on in visual culture.

Now that music genres have been unhitched from the centralised broadcast media, and now genre labels are not ordered through TV, weeklies and radio, the possibilities have suddenly opened for music to be ordered in new ways. One of the key changes here is that music cultures are now largely self-organising. Genre labels might still be dreamed up and created by industry insiders, journalists and artists, but they are also the product of interaction through social media and with streaming playlists and so on. The tagging and playlisting processes that are used to classify music are now performed and attached by those with an interest in consuming the music as well as those involved in its production and distribution. This has opened up the potential for music genres to proliferate, expand and develop, for sub genres and even sub-sub-sub genres to spiral, and on other occasions for genres judged irrelevant to wither into the background.

The result of this new type of musical categorisation is that music cultures become self-organising things. This self-organising system is open to rapid change, to increasingly granular and microscopic genres (and genres within genres), and to the fragmenting of musical categories around small differences. To understand music, and platform cultures more generally, we need to focus a little more on how these cultures are organising themselves.

This is a revealing set of practices that tell us much about how people identify with culture, how they differentiate their tastes and themselves from other people and how culture can be understood as it becomes a part of people's lives. Here we have something close to collective classificatory work. Real-time, on-demand and social media enable responsive classifications of everyday culture. I have focussed upon music here, but this is now touching lots of cultural spheres. Viewed from the point of view of music genre we are likely to feel quite disorientated, yet attempting to understand the new genre formations as decentralised classificatory systems is really instructive and revealing. Either way, it is hard to conclude anything except that music genre has become something much more complex and varied, the catalyst for this was the increasing involvement of the listeners in the categorisation of the music that they like on the one hand, and the vast escalation of content available on the other. Perhaps then this tells us something about how people consume culture and how they use genre categories to differentiate their tastes and to mark out a sense of individualised identity. It might also suggest something of the ordering processes that are going on in platform-based cultures and how people are managing the deluge of content. Yet these self-organising systems are not just about the human actors involved in shaping the order of things, there are also processes of automation at work. We might wonder what power algorithms have in the automated ordering of culture.

WHY IS EVERYONE TALKING ABOUT ALGORITHMS?

Just before midnight on the 6 October 2016 the GB pound suddenly dropped by 6% before recovering most of that lost value during the early hours of the morning. Theories circulated about how this might have happened.[41] Was it a product of a typo in a trade or some other similar mishap, or was it the result of some unknown activity amongst the many algorithms that are involved in such trading? Whatever the answers, algorithms became the most likely culprit. Something similar happened with the previous 'flash crash' of 2010. Since the reports of the apparent manipulation of Facebook's news feed algorithms covered in 2014,[42] news stories about algorithms have become frequent. Algorithms seem to be taking on an increasing public profile. The concern is often with what these algorithms or even *Westworld*-style 'rogue algorithms'[43] might be doing to us. One result of these highly visible twists is that code is no longer considered to be solely the interest of software developers, hackers or computer enthusiasts.[44] Instead, an interest in algorithms is now becoming something of a mainstream pastime. As a result of our intrigue with their powers, algorithms are becoming something of an icon of our data-dense and software enacted lives.

   Despite isolating algorithms as a potential source of this sudden crash in the pound, the accounts remain inconclusive. No one is quite sure exactly what happened. Which is revealing in itself. It shows that these systems have become so complex that they are almost incomprehensible. They are a bundle of lots of systems serving lots of interests as they activate trades, measure sentiment and pre-empt market fluctuations. Back in 2002 Stephen Graham and Simon Marvin outlined the processes that they described as 'splintering urbanism'.[45] Their book was concerned with understanding the vast systems that overlap and make-up urban spaces. The many overlapping service providers, utilities and commercial infrastructures of the city, they argue, mean that they have splintered and become almost impossible to know or fully understand. It would seem that the algorithmic systems linked to this 'flash crash' are following these broader splintering processes. The splintered complexity of the different algorithms, codes and systems means that collectively they are unknowable. We might be able to understand one part, but the whole will always be elusive.

The fact that this happens without it being possible to put together a full explanation of this flash crash of the 6 October 2016 suggests that a similar splintering process is happening within the mediated social world more broadly – there are just too many things going on that might feed into such an event and too many splintered systems. On top of this, we can then add Frank Pasquale's popular notion of the 'Black Box Society',[46] in which we are largely unaware of the algorithmic led processes that act upon us. The algorithm then, or algorithms operating in various combinations, resides within a collective 'technological unconscious', as Nigel Thrift once described it.[47] The fascination with algorithms might be a consequence then of their apparently powerful effects, like being able to radically devalue currency without any warning, whilst they remain largely unknowable and elusive. They have splintered into combinations of which the outcomes are unpredictable and impossible to unpick.

In terms of our growing interest and the rising volume of news stories, algorithms are likely to be appealing because of the very fact that they appear both enigmatic and mysterious whilst seeming powerful and assertive. Algorithms provoke much commentary, they are said to 'rule our working lives',[48] to 'rule the world'[49] to perpetuate prejudice[50] and to potentially manipulate us[51] or make us 'slaves'.[52] It's not just what is being said about algorithms that matters, but just how prominent they are becoming in media coverage (as I will discuss a bit more in a moment). There is a steady flow of news and comment about algorithms. Mysteries are always of interest, especially when they are mysteries that directly shape our lives.

On the one hand then, algorithms are active in making recommendations to us about what to read, what to watch, what to listen to, who to hire, what risks to take, how we might exercise, who we might connect with on social media and so on. And these algorithms are, of course central to how culture is encountered and consumed. They are active in border, risk and security decisions,[53] or in insurance and financial service decisions.

They filter news feeds, prioritise searches define what is encountered and when. The list goes on. This is only the tip of a very big iceberg, especially as algorithms are deployed to take advantage of the unfathomable quantity of data produced about people. So, one reason why algorithms are now being spoken about so frequently is that they are so active within our lives.[54] The influence or 'social power of algorithms' has become hard to ignore.[55]

The *notion of the algorithm* is also becoming really quite powerful in its own right. The very idea of what an algorithm is and what it can do has taken on a life of its own, especially in the popular media. Algorithms are becoming the shadowy figures that in some way embody wider fears and concerns. The visions we have of algorithms chime with broader feelings of a loss of control, of accelerated lives that are speeding away from us, of our inability to cope with the unmanageable information that we are exposed to, or the feeling that our lives are governed for us and that we have less discretion, autonomy or voice.

The talk about algorithms is a product of the powerful role that they now have in our lives, but the talk around algorithms also seems to tap into broader concerns about powerlessness and the limitations placed on our discretion and choice. The algorithm is coming to embody the sense of life as out of our control. Algorithms are evoked to speak to these fears and concerns. This is not to say that they don't have material influences on our lives, they clearly have profound consequences. But the idea of the algorithm is also now a powerful presence, jumping out suddenly from the mass of code within which everyday life is lived to give us the occasional fright or to remind us of our sense of limited autonomy.

These enigmas of the splintering data rich society are likely to grow in their profile and notoriety in the coming years. Especially as fears of the unknowability of the forces acting upon us continue to unfold in ways that we can't fully comprehend. The 'flash crash' is one moment in which the algorithm emerges from the shadows, but these moments are becoming more frequent. The figure of the algorithm is likely to be something we will encounter more frequently as their mysteries unfold, as our interest is piqued and as we continue to experience algorithmic processes impinging on upon us. The reach of algorithms in culture is particularly advanced, given the way that culture is mediated by these platforms and their algorithmic sorting, filtering and prioritisation.

ALGORITHMS AS HEROES AND VILLAINS

Over the last two years, discussion of 'post-truth' has been everywhere.[56]. Questions about the status of truth and fact in political debate have acquired a pre-eminence in commentaries on the complex political developments of recent years. These stories vary, but they share an understandable concern with the consequences of misinformation. Which, of course, are far-reaching.

Within this debate, algorithms have taken on a surprising presence, often as the source of blame for affording the conditions in which lies and manipulated 'facts' can thrive. Alongside the emergence of notions of the 'post-truth' era, however accurate that might be, algorithms have increased in public profile and level of notoriety.

As many accounts of the last year have made clear, social media now play a powerful role in shaping the circulation of news and information. The recent reports and wide-ranging reflection concerning the sharing of 'fake news'[57] on Facebook are part of broader claims that social media provide the perfect conditions for the propagation and dissemination of misinformation. As we know, it was even suggested that this sharing of 'fake news' on social media influenced decision-making during elections.[58] In general terms, what we are beginning to see here is what happens to news when the decentralisation of media takes hold. News and current affairs were dominated by broadcast media and newspapers as little as 10 years ago.[59] Now decentralised forms of social media change not just the way that such information spreads but also how it is produced. As I have already discussed, we have masses of content held in self-organising media archives.

One outcome of this in recent political cultures is that Facebook and other social media are seen to be enabling new kinds of 'post-truth politics' to flourish[60] – which has become a dominant trope and cause for concern. This has recently been linked to the already established idea of a social media 'filter bubble',[61] in which we are exposed to views and information that reinforce existing world views.[62] Social media algorithms are envisioned as locking us in or hermetically sealing us off from alternative perspectives, whilst also making us more likely to believe potential misinformation that fits within existing ideas of the world (which I will return to in the final chapter of this book).

This is comparable with the kind of 'bubbling'[63] that we see within the social world more broadly, with people seeking to withdraw or to 'pad the bunker'[64] – from gated communities[65] to the use of smartphones or earphones.[66] Social media might appear to be a site of connection and networking, but it has long been argued that internet-based media forms produce a kind of 'networked individualism'.[67] The difference with social media is that the infrastructures themselves manage our networks, shape our newsfeeds and filter the masses of content into the things we are most likely to want to see.

Perhaps the most significant change we are seeing here concerns the new types of politics of circulation[68] that underpin the transformations that social media bring. Information circulates around social media at an alarming rate, afforded by the tagging of content and the algorithms that sort and prioritise. News agendas move quickly. It can be possible for people to anticipate what will circulate and to use these social media to gain rapid visibility for their points. Such visibility is possible for those who know how to tag the news with metadata and who have a sense of how algorithms might then enable the sharing to snowball. In short, those with the capacity, money and capabilities to use social media's politics of circulation to their advantage are most likely to get heard.

As with everything else that happens in social media, news and information become a means for provoking activity. These are the conditions in which information and misinformation now circulate, in a space aimed at *prediction rather than curation*. Of course, all of this is now quite familiar. Because of the role of algorithms in news circulation they have become the villains of the piece.

On the occasion that the human team[69] was reportedly removed from monitoring Facebook trends, it was reported that the algorithmic processes were not as discerning in differentiating the quality or accuracy or background agendas of the news delivered to people. Algorithms took on a malevolent character in these stories, and in the so-called post-truth era that they embodied. The 'echo chamber' or 'filter bubble' perspectives also suggested that algorithms were responsible for sealing people off from visions of the world that contravened or challenged their own. Algorithms' villainous status continued to grow. They now not only failed to filter the rubbish out, they also enabled spurious and dangerous content to amplify whilst closing down world-views.[70]

Algorithms now have a material presence in shaping the social world in often unseen ways. It is interesting that the notion of 'post-truth' has also had the effect of increasing the public profile of algorithms and their embedded presence – particularly in social media. In a brilliant piece of analysis, Ben Williamson has shown how the media coverage of algorithms varies between media outlets.[71] The variations in positive and negative coverage are striking. So your perspective on the merits or destructive capacity of algorithms may well depend on your reading patterns.

It is the proposed solution to the impact of these media forms that has conversely pitched the algorithm as the potential saviour. With developments around algorithms being used to check facts in real-time,[72] allowing utterances and content to be examined at scale and instantly, the vision of the algorithm becomes more heroic. The only way to resolve the problems created by algorithms, it would seem, is to counter them with more algorithms. This is often what we find in the discourse of tech providers, the answer is always to increase the density and reach of the tech.

The result is that algorithms are depicted as both the villains and potential heroes of these so-called 'post-truth' politics. They might enable lies and misinformation to successfully circulate, but in the context of what Mark Andrejevic has called the 'infoglut'[73] they are also then suggested to provide the only real means for spotting the problems in the unfathomable masses of information. This instant type of analytics is close to what Andrejevic describes as the pursuit of 'immediation'. They can appear to cut out the need for the extensive mediation of content. Through a kind of real-time fact checking, algorithms can then be said to save the day – or that is, save us from the problems created by other algorithms.

The question is whether we think more algorithms can solve the malaise and remove the problems of bypassing a discerning editorial eye. It's unclear how to resolve this, but the close alignment between algorithms and so-called 'post-truth' suggests something. As the profile of algorithms has grown and as their actions become the source of discussion, we might want to avoid thinking of them as good and bad algorithms, and think instead about how these media forms mesh human with machine agency – this will allow us to focus on what these transformations mean for culture and information. Reducing it to algorithms as the problem and/or solution might cause us to miss just how much of the decision-making and visibility is in the hands of code.

Whether we see algorithms as villains or heroes (or both), what really matters is how those algorithms are used and deployed to shape who and what gets heard in the mutating public sphere. At the very least we need to think about whether the apparent problems created by algorithms can be resolved with more algorithms. The problem with treating algorithms as heroes or villains is that it might distract us – in the same way that we might be distracted by the concept of post-truth itself – from how power is being deployed through those algorithms.

CULTURAL ACCELERATION 1: THE CLOSURE OF VINE

So far this chapter has looked at how classificatory systems are being reshaped, how self-organising systems have emerged and the role of algorithms in shaping cultural encounters. This, I am suggesting, gives us a little glimpse into the ordering processes of the cultural landscape. Together these give an impression of the shifting nature of the order of things within platform orientated digital cultures. Within these changing systems the above sections have hinted at some shifts in temporality. The instant and immediate connections with culture and with ranked classifications and the like undoubtedly brings changes to the speed of our connections and consumption. I am going to now pick out just two illustrative examples that hint at how these shifting structures can also be understood in terms of cultural acceleration. These don't tell the full story, but are suggestive of the direction of change in digital culture. The two examples are the closure of Vine and the cultural shifts suggested by the music charts.

Vine, the micro-video-blogging service launched in 2012 announced its impending closure in late 2016.[74] It only existed for a short time, yet its impact was of some significance. With its six-second video clips, Vine was at the forefront of the field when it came to adding video content to social media. The baton has been picked up by various places since, with video embedded more centrally in many of the leading social media formats. A key issue was that other platforms came to facilitate and incorporate this type of visual content rendering Vine increasingly redundant.

As can be seen by the popularity of image led sites such Instagram, in the decade or so since social media has become embedded in everyday life it has become increasingly visual. The creative content generated has shifted towards capturing the users' visual imagination – and as we know the visual can be consumed much more quickly than text. Memes, which invite participation, are now a prominent means of communication around shared ideas, and represent a form of communicative play, drawing users in as these visual jokes and comments mutate and grow (before, usually, dying out).[75]

So social media have become more visual and instant in their form, along with this they have also become more conducive to rapid consumption of content – trends that Vine encapsulated. Vine's video content used imagery and its short videos to quickly capture attention, whilst the six-second limit meant that the site was designed with speed in mind. Short bits of content consumed rapidly and shared easily. However, the end of Vine did not signal the end of these trends – Vine's closure was more to do with the power of competitors like Snapchat offering much the same and cost-saving staff cuts at Twitter,[76] its parent company, than it was to do with a lack of enthusiasm for what it offered. In any case, much of Vine's video-posting functionality has been built into Twitter itself.[77] It was not a change in direction for social media but an escalation of the properties that Vine embodied that then subsequently created problems for it.

We are living in what appear to be accelerated times – as sociologist Judy Wajcman put it recently, we feel 'pressed for time'.[78] The argument here is that our lives seem to be shaped by the speed and volume of the information to which we are exposed. The trends towards the visual and speediness continue.

Commentators, from media theorist Mark Andrejevic[79] to stand-up comedian Dave Gorman,[80] have suggested that our everyday lives are defined by the feeling that we are experiencing too much information. This overloading effect alters how we question and understand the world – and even, as we have seen has been suggested, a grasp of the truth.[81] So social media will be likely to unfold along the lines of these broader social trends, striving to operate more quickly in order to give people the opportunity to keep up with a rapidly changing world.

Scott Lash claims that this deluge has drastically escalated in recent years. He has argued that we now live in an 'intensive culture' marked by rapid rhythms and a high density of information.[82] As global networks spread outwards they also press inwards upon us, he argues, broadening in scope whilst also ramping up the intensity and concentration they exert on us.[83] This applies to anything, from binge-watching television boxsets to the torrents of social media posts. Everyday experience is much more tightly packed with stuff.

It is possible to see social media as fuelling what cultural theorist John Tomlinson has referred to as the 'cultures of speed'.[84] Social media might well be one of the things that makes life seem quicker, but at the same time the feeling that we are 'pressed for time' in turn shapes how people use these platforms. In this context visual forms of communication become more appealing, predominantly because they allow us to communicate and share ideas more rapidly. So Vine's pursuit of the visual and the rapid continues even though Vine will not. Social media is likely to continue with its trend towards more visual and more instant forms of content and communication.

CULTURAL ACCELERATION 2: DEBUT NUMBER 1S AND THE ACCELERATING POP CHART

In early September 1994 Whigfield released her single '*Saturday Night*'. It was the pre-internet era equivalent of a viral hit – the dance moves to accompany the song had been published in the newspapers. It appeared from nowhere and echoed everywhere. As songs go it seemed quite innocuous. But its catchy wafer-thin sound actually represented a watershed moment in music chart history.

When it displaced Wet Wet Wet's 15-week stay at the top with '*Love is All Around*', Whigfield's '*Saturday Night*' became the first ever debut single to go straight into the charts at number one. The UK singles sales chart had originally launched in 1952, so it took more than 40 years of weekly charts for this to happen. For 40 years, artists had been trying to build momentum and use broadcast media outlets and publicity drives to push their songs steadily up the charts. But Whigfield struck gold immediately.

If we glimpse back to 2014 we find something interesting. Given this history of the music charts, it might be surprising to discover that in 2014 as many as 14 different acts achieved a number one with their debut single. So we had 40 years without a number one debut single, years that saw releases from a wide array of cultural luminaries – and in 2014 alone we had 14 in a single year. And 2014 isn't an isolated case.

So where did the so called 'year of the debut chart smash'[85] come from? Clearly in part the evolving way in which music is consumed, some of which I have already discussed, is relevant in this. Chart rules have changed over recent years in order to accommodate changes in music formats and to make the charts representative of the actual music being consumed.

The changes are almost too numerous to list, but in 2006 music downloads were included in the charts for the first time, enabling Gnarls Barkley's single 'Crazy' to be the first single to reach number one on downloads alone (the CD format was released after it had first charted). And then in 2014, streamed music began to be included in the calculation of chart position, 100 streams of a song counting as a single sale.[86] The changes continued. All of this leads to changes in the outcomes of the charts and the form they take.

As already outlined, the pace of music culture was also quite different before social media formats took off. Information about music can spread much more quickly now. The weekly chart was indicative of the previously slower pace. Music news travelled through broadcast media outlets, such as magazines, weekly music newspapers, radio and so on. Periodic and slow, they have been usurped by the constant and instant cultural viewpoints found today. Even in the 1990s, the emergence of the internet did little to speed up music cultures – although as I will show in a moment 1998 was a threshold moment.

Today's music movements are undoubtedly accelerating, particularly as social media has become an integral part of music culture. This is perhaps another example that is illustrative of a broader cultural speed-up, with information passing quickly between people and through their expansive social networks. In marketing terms, this is about the buzz.

In the case of Whigfield the news of the dance routine associated with the song helped in whipping up a buzz, foreshadowing the release of the single and easing it to number one in its first week. Today various social media outlets enable the buzz around artists to grow more rapidly and to spread quickly. As a result, artists can become very well-known before they have even released their first single, so more of them are able to go straight to number one. Music streaming sites neatly link the buzz around artists to listening practices, allowing people to listen to the artists that are gaining momentum – the buzz is amplified.

The ways in which music consumption has changed is important but we need to consider the shifts of the platforms underpinning culture and the speed at which culture is now able to spread. The pace at which information circulates is much quicker than it was in the past and the rhythms of cultural consumption have changed as a result.

But this frenzied listening culture has another side – if music movements explode quickly they are also likely to burn out. In 2014 the number one single changed 41 times. Yes, there were some singles that reached the top on more than one occasion, such as Pharrell Williams's '*Happy*' and Mark Ronson's '*Uptown Funk*', but this is still a rapid turnover. Only six of these singles managed to maintain their number one position for more than one week.

If we look at the charts in the 1950s and 1960s for comparison, we find that the number one single often changed less than 20 times in a year – with a few artists dominating. The top spot is now changing very frequently and we are seeing a wider range of artists achieving recognition in a single year: this is musical turnover at a rate that we have never seen before.

Capitalism has always had its rapid turnover of goods and mobile trends, but it looks like platform culture is increasingly defined by a concerted speed-up that is likely to be followed by burn-out and fade-away. Songs and other cultural forms will arrive from nowhere and disappear quickly – we see this with the way memes arrive quickly and fade rapidly. Popular culture has always moved with haste, but we might see even more one-hit wonders and quickly forgotten artists. Perhaps this is one explanation for the re-emergence and growing popularity of vinyl – a small act of resistance to cultural speed-up and a tangible object that gives some sense of permanence to music's dizzying movements. It might also be part of the reason for the frequent comebacks that have typified recent years (which I will return to in Chapter 4).

It is possible to add some further context to this year of debut number ones, there are other traces of acceleration of pop culture in the charts. Launched in November 1952, as I have mentioned, the official UK music charts have acted as a barometer of taste. As well as measuring popularity, the charts act as a kind of archive of the songs that have defined the soundscapes of different times. Beyond revealing and ranking the popularity of a song in a given week, taken as a whole the charts can also tell us something else: how quickly pop moves and shifts.

Looking back at particular moments in chart history gives us a flavour of the fashions and trends, but the charts also contain underlying patterns. One story they can tell is of the speed-up of changes in pop culture. One way of seeing this acceleration is to look at number one singles over time.[87] When it comes to looking at the charts, there is quite a bit of variation across the individual years, with some popular songs staying at number one for an extended period and, of course, the ephemera of the one-hit-wonder and so on. Looking at the average number of number ones in different decades gives a better sense of the underlying patterns, rather than the momentary shifts.[88]

The picture we get is of music taste, in the form it is represented in weekly charts at least, shifting quite radically. There was only a single number one in 1952, Al Martino's *Here in My Heart*. It arrived at number one in the week the charts were launched and stayed there for nine weeks – a steady start that set a leisurely pace for the years that immediately followed. In the 1950s, the average number of number one hits per year was 14. By the 2010s this had increased, doubled in fact, to 28. So, on average the 2010s saw 14 more number ones per year than the 1950s. The turnover today, as we might expect, is much quicker than in those early chart years. In fact, the pace accelerated a little in the 1960s, jumping up to an average of 19 number ones per year. The big-act pop enthusiasm and exploding youth cultures of the 1960s slowed a little again in the 1970s with a drop to 17, before accelerating back up to 19 in the 1980s.

The real change arrived in the 1990s. As music culture itself moved towards being more fragmented, so too the charts became more volatile. The 1990s had an average of 21 number ones per year, yet this number is a little misleading. The 1990s started fairly steadily, holding back the average, but it picked up pace in 1996 before the real turning point arrived in 1998, when there were 32 number ones in a year. The pace stepped up again with 36 number ones in 1999. This pattern continued, hitting an all-time high of 42 number ones in the year 2000 – a number that has never been beaten, although it was repeated in 2014. The average for the 2000s was a jump up to 28, which was then replicated in the 2010s. The charts suggest that the pace of change in music cultures was growing fairly steadily up until that point in 1998 when things really started to come and go much more quickly – with some obvious and fairly limited exceptions where big stars have had number ones for multiple weeks. The internet, which really started to take hold in 1998, is likely to have provided that extra gear in the acceleration of turnover in pop. There are lots of other explanations as to why the music charts are accelerating. The changing of the chart rules is one – but these have tended to reflect rather than lead changes in cultural consumption. Whichever way we understand this, the relative impermanency and the greater range of access in music streaming is important. And, of course, capitalism is founded upon the increase in demand for new goods; perhaps we are just seeing such processes being refined and these impulses driven further. Although, of course, acceleration has certainly not helped music industry revenues, which have dropped sub-stantially since the 1990s and are only just now begging to see comparable increases.

What is most striking though is that the trend towards acceleration seems to have been defied in the last three years. The year 2016 saw the lowest ever number of number ones in a single year in chart history, with only 11. This low point was followed by 17 and 19 in 2017 and 2018 respectively. This might be a blip in the apparent cultural acceleration, or it might suggest a slowing down. This apparent slow-down since 2016 is a bit harder to explain, especially as it seems to reverse the trend. Writing about clothing in the early 1900s, the sociologist Georg Simmel argued that the more rapid the changes in fashion the more 'nervous' was the age.[89] If this also applies to music trends, then we might have expected the upheaval of the last couple of years to have sped up the charts rather than slowing them down.

It's hard to be certain, but the charts reveal something of the change in the speed with which music shifts around. Perhaps what we are looking at is the type of chart that emerges as music consumption becomes more eclectic and diverse, with only certain artists possessing the clout to get heard and the obduracy to defy the rapid tides of music culture that we have experienced since the late 1990s. Maybe the slow-down of the last three years is a product of the systems through which music is consumed (and the cultural ordering I have already gestured towards).

Our attention is being guided towards certain artists and certain songs by streaming services. A possible result of this is that focus narrows, like in the pre-internet era, on prominent songs, and so we have fewer number ones per year. This poses a question about the way that music rises to the top in the current media landscape and how social media and music streaming might seem individualised whilst drawing the collective atten-tion towards certain tracks. It is possible that what we are seeing here is the tension that occurs between cultural acceleration and eclecticism on one hand and the way that algorithmic systems seek to draw attention in certain directions (as discussed earlier in this chapter).

CONCLUSION

It would seem that aspects of everyday life are getting quicker, or appear to be quicker at least, whilst the categories and classifications used to order culture are also proliferating as people seek to make sense of things and cope with the vastness of cultural content. We can imagine here that *a new order of things* is beginning to emerge on these platforms, with implications for the way that culture is encountered and consumed. We experience culture within these layered systems of classification. Hashtags, playlists and other cross-cutting classificatory systems render the world consumable to us in accessible ways and bring a new kind of energy and distributed knowledge to cultural experience. These self-organising systems blend together human and machine agency along with commercially and individually demarcated classification. What I have called elsewhere a 'classificatory imagination'[90] is unlocked as culture moves onto these tech platforms. Not only do social media hashtags and other forms of tagging and playlisting rely upon active classificatory practices, they also call upon a creative engagement with those classifications. Coming up with classifications has also become a pass-time in itself and is often as important as the content. A witty or creative label for the content is a part of how these cultures operate.

Beyond these levels of participatory classification emerging in social media, the ordering of culture takes a more passive but nonetheless expansive form in other spaces. When choosing a film, TV show, music, book or game, we are now presented with categories and labels that stretch far beyond the genre titles that we might have experienced in the past. Take Netflix for example, here cultural forms are not simply drama, thriller and so on, rather they come with creative and focussed labels that capture various properties. The labels used on these dashboards are dynamic and changeable; grouping content and presenting it back to us in innumerable constellations of entertainment. These category labels are ever changing, giving us the archive over and over again in different forms through this vast range of classificatory headers.

If we take social media's ordering principles, it is perhaps *the feed* that is most dominant. The unending flow of content across the screen as we move ever downwards through it. These feeds are curated but limitless – prioritised but indefinite. Feeds are hierarchies of content, sorted for us into priority order, but they also continue to unfold. From search results, to recommendations of videos and the like, unending personalised music or video automated playback, to social media news feeds, they are a dominant mode of engagement that shape the ordering of culture. The feed is defined by it having no endpoint. We flick ever downwards. Trapped by these sticky feeds and what we might miss out on if we don't hold on to see whatever lies beyond the edges of the screen. The promise of the next downswipe holds us in. Stopping is a wrench and so these media flourish off the back of our sustained activity. It is easy to be mesmerised by the lapping waves of content breaking in front of us. When thinking of the order of things, as I have tried to do in this chapter, it is often *the feed* that shapes our encounters with cultural content.

The complexity and diversity of platform culture means that ordering is of significant importance to the way culture is experienced. This ordering is dynamic and has a temporality, it is not fixed or slow, but is in tension and constant animation. As the ordering of culture has changed, so too has the way that we find and relate to content. The classification of culture is always something people have been active in, it is just that the creation and interpretation of the new and expanding classificatory systems of culture is so much more lively, varied and participatory. Ordering has become more directly a part of the cultures themselves, with us actively engaging in creating, using and attempting to apply these ordering systems ourselves. This process is particularly notable where the increasingly visual and instant forms that culture takes become reflected in the instant labelling processes to which that content is exposed. The ordering of culture has been disrupted, and a vastly different and imaginative set of processes is now emerging. In platform culture, classification is much closer to the surface in cultural experiences than it has been before. Like the cultural forms themselves, the ordering of culture is also more instant, visual and rapid.

3

TOTAL RECALL: THE PAST, PRESENT AND FUTURE

The ability to access content from different periods, instantly, means that the platforming of culture is transforming the relations between past, present and future. In particular, the way that we consume the past is shifting as the platforms that we use change their form. As I will discuss in a moment, social media have become memory devices, giving us our own past back in digestible but detailed forms. This is just one aspect of a changing set of relations with the past and with our own biographies. It is hard to see where this stops or even where it begins. The fact that we have lived with social media and mobile devices for over a decade means that the archiving potential they bring changes the way we relate to shared and individual histories. In this chapter, I will explore some of these dynamics, but like so many of the topics I am exploring in this book, the possibilities and issues far outstrip the points I begin to develop here. Even if we just take the broader changes I am describing in this book, covering around a decade or so, we also have to think about the way that those very changes are premised upon a particular view of the past. I will start though by thinking about how digital culture also allows us to explore and consume the past in new ways.

BECOMING MEDIA SAVVY: TV GAME SHOWS AND SOCIAL CHANGE

The jokes are usually about the speedboats. And, granted, it is funny when two people seemingly bewildered by what use it might have been to them, are shown a speedboat that they have just failed to win. But there is something revealing about the comedic response we have to old TV game shows like *Bullseye*.[91] As they are recalled in nostalgic laments of memory or through the repeats made available on digital TV, these old game shows evoke the distance of time and an ironic sense of whim for the way we were 30 years ago. With the distance of time, there is something quaint and even strange about these shows. This was a time, if we believe what we are seeing, when people could win a metal tankard or a handmade key fob without a crushing sense of awkward self-awareness or the need to look into the camera lens to share the joke. These shows act as a portal on the passage of cultural-time, they present to us a society that seems quite distant, alien and maybe even odd: the palette of beige and grey, the neon lights, the captions –'jackpot', 'holiday of a lifetime', 'a family fortune of ...', 'TVs biggest...' – the posing models, the multipurpose sets, the applause, the innuendo, the grinning hosts and the catchphrases. I have often thought that you could use TV game shows as documents of social change, they seem to capture something of their time. Over recent years the UK Freeview channel Challenge has provided plenty of opportunity to reflect on this thesis. This channel predominantly shows old episodes of TV game shows from the 1980s and early 1990s (although it has expanded its coverage to more recent and new programmes in recent times). This was something of a golden era for this type of TV format. Challenge has shown old episodes of a wide variety of shows including *Bullseye*, *Family Fortunes*, *Take Your Pick*, *Big Break*, *The Price Is Right*, *Strike it Lucky*, *Celebrity Squares*, *321* and *Wheel of Fortune*. If we look carefully, these repeats potentially reveal more than a taste for nostalgia, they actually document some interesting social characteristics of the time – especially when compared to the few equivalent programmes of today.

Game shows today, if we can still call them that, are often centred on large cash prizes, a million pounds is often the landmark but it is nearly always in the tens-of-thousands at least. Although in some cases the prizes are knowingly small, and are delivered with an unmissable sense of irony and a calculated wink (*Pointless* deploys this type of approach). Back in the 1980s shows like *Bullseye* were built around prizes, these prizes might be seen to reveal something of the aspirations of the time. There is an overwhelming sameness to the desired lifestyles that are put on display and narrated by these prizes: from pine plant stands and canteens of cutlery to trouser presses and hand-held video cameras. And then there are the infrequently won star prizes: a trailer tent, a caravan, a fitted kitchen, a dining room suite, a hatchback and a speed boat. These prizes all reveal something of the aspirations of the time, they may even say something of lifestyle choices and perhaps even social mobility. On *Wheel of Fortune* we see something similar, with a pint size bottle of French perfume contained in a large glass flower, leather trouser suits and 'his and hers' watches. These are prizes that seem to be woven with powerful social norms – embodied by those 'his and hers' watches.

If we look across the TV games shows I have listed above, we begin to get a vision of what might have been an ideal or utopian lifestyle to-be-desired. Waking up to a cup of tea prepared by an automatic teasmade, preparing a fondue in a fitted kitchen, entertaining around a barbeque whilst sitting on garden furniture and sipping from a magnum of champagne poured into champagne flutes, or perhaps gathered around a dining room table serving from a hostess trolley to a table decked in gold knives and forks whilst discussing our latest holiday of a lifetime – then our guests, dressed in Italian leather jackets, drive their saloon cars home for a nightcap poured from a cut-glass decanter. These are the types of dream lifestyles that are woven into the prizes and into the way that these objects are presented to the contestants and viewers. They have norms bound up within them, norms that now might appear stifling in their depiction of the lifestyles that they are scripted to be a part of. These shows, many of which were watched by very large audiences, seem to say something about the types of *want* that were dominant at the time, and may even be a precursor to the types of visions of consumerism we see today. The prizes in 1980s and 1990s game shows were about scripted lifestyles but today's are about the consumer freedoms of money. That is to say that instead of pre-determined objects with narratives and norms attached to them, the focus is now upon the limitless possibilities of large sums of cash.

Looking back at these shows though what is perhaps most immediately obvious is how the protagonists have become much more media savvy. We now appear to innately understand how to behave on the television. Contestants of the 1980s and 1990s appear unsure and uncomfortable. They are uncertain in their movements and often mumble their way through anecdotes, furtively looking at their shoes. They appear to be wearing the clothes they would wear to work or when at home – this is the colour palette of greys and light browns that contrast with the brightly coloured sets. They appear to be ill prepared for the experience. The knowledge of how to *be media content* is not yet developed. Somewhere along the line we became more media savvy, with the confidence to speak, dress and move in the way expected and required of a TV persona. The contestants may no longer be dressing themselves but, if this is indeed the case, they look comfortable in the retrofit clothes provided by the stylists. People appearing on TV no longer appear out of place or like they are participating in a disconcerting or traumatic adventure to the unknown. They appear to know what they are doing. It is like we are now media trained as a routine part of our socialisation processes. In the 1980s game shows in particular, and a little in the game shows of the 1990s, there is still something of the wonderment in what Graeme Turner has described as the presence of 'ordinary people' in the media and a 'demotic turn'.[92] It is as if both the contestants and the viewers are surprised that they are a part of what is happening. They respond accordingly. This is no longer the case, the wonderment has passed, contestants and other demotic protagonists today look increasingly like they belong – and the viewers are not surprised to see them there. We have become more used to being watched and broadcast.

These old TV game shows are not the type of documents or artefacts that might usually be used by those interested in understanding social change, but there is definitely a rich resource here, a kind of audio and visual account and archive of these times. I remember once visiting an art installation that simply included a TV displaying a short loop of an old game show based around a variety of pub games. There was no narrative or text, the artist appeared to be inviting the visitor to reflect back on this historical artefact. These old TV game shows tell surprising stories and reveal something of the time. These are audio and visual documents that depict social change. There is definitely more to be said, but for the moment they certainly seem to say something about aspiration and about how we have become increasingly media savvy. Social media provides a platform to practice *being media content*, so TV appearances are experienced in the context of that training. As well as a contrast with the comfort of contestants on today's TV equivalents, this shift becomes most obvious when we compare the media personas of those in reality TV and structured reality shows – from *The Kardashians* to *The Only Way is Essex* – to those contestants on *Bullseye*. We have cultivated a media savviness that permeates right through digital culture.

THOSE MATTER OUT OF PLACE MOMENTS

Beige Jacket. Shoulder pads. Gold shiny tie. Immaculate quiff. Smug expression. A neutral peach-flecked backdrop. Jonathan Ross slips into one of his smooth segues. It was the summer of 1991. Ross introduces Nirvana who, he tells us, are going to play *Lithium* 'yes, sir, indeed'. A part the set lifts up revealing Nirvana – they launch into *Territorial Pissings*.

This has long been one of my favourite TV music moments. I didn't see the live performance; I came across the clip on my VHS video copy of *Nirvana Live! Tonight! Sold Out!!* It's not just that they switch song nor is it simply that they play a raw version of the least commercial song on their album *Nevermind*, it is the contrast between them, their sound and their setting. They race through the song, finishing it and promptly walking off to a cacophony of feedback, unsettling a few bits of equipment on the way. Leaving the audience audibly bemused. Cut back to Ross for another smooth segue and cheeky comment. It's the contrast between the setting and the band that makes it such a great moment. The slickness of the show is juxtaposed with the rough edges of the band. It's a famous clip, but it still carries some of the drama and sense of disruption that it represents. Nirvana, despite being a big commercially successful band looked like matter out of place on mainstream TV.

This is far from a unique moment. There are lots of times when bands or artists have appeared on TV and looked out of place, like they don't quite fit with the surroundings. There would occasionally be a mater-out-of-place type performance amongst the bopping glitz of *Top of the Pops*. A band might show up to play their single on a breakfast TV show, a daytime magazine programme, a talk show or maybe at some awards ceremony or other, whilst not quite belonging with the scene. We have probably all got our own lists. These moments where the music is out of place lend a heightened sense of an alternative culture. The contrast serves to make that particular featured act seem even more different than they might otherwise seem. Glistening against the banality. The contrast emphasises the idea that the music is somehow subcultural – even if, like with Nirvana, it is actually not that far from the mainstream, just in a different form. The sense of alternative culture is more pronounced where it comes into the orbit of the things it is not. These are points where different cultural movements, with their own rules and norms, clash together.

Giving a sense of their cultural presence, these types of out of place performances even found their way into the first episode of the spoof TV chat show *Knowing Me, Knowing You with Alan Partridge*, which was broadcast about three years after the Nirvana performance. In that episode an imaginary punk band provide a disruptive performance that contrasts with the straight-laced TV format and presenter. The fact that these moments could be replicated on a spoof TV comedy suggests that they are enough of a familiar presence for the joke to make sense. They were clearly an occasional if not common occurrence. These types of moments had to be regular enough for this reference to work. With the spoof, as with the actual cases, it is the disruption and the disturbance to the usual running of culture that makes it work.

The visual parts of music culture are now much stronger and more dynamic than they were then. Artists can create and share their own videos much more easily, then there are the many live performances that are captured, and we can even go back and re-watch those old moments like the Nirvana TV appearance. We now have vast audio visual archives of music cultures past and present. This enables a much more vibrant and diverse visual side to music culture than we have had prior to the last few years. Alongside this, music on the main TV channels has changed its presence. The talk show format has changed, either going late night or excluding live music performances. The rare occasions of live performances on TV are unlikely to go beyond quite choreographed performances from carefully curated artists – either that or they are restricted to dedicated live music TV shows where such performances would belong anyway, and which are again late night watching. As a result, it seems we are less likely to get these rare moments of contrast, there is less matter out of place. Cultural consumption has become more fragmented, with greater diversity but with fewer opportunities for crossovers between these cultural streams.

The visual side to music has evolved and adapted as it has become much more decentralised, opening opportunities for creativity and for different ways of complementing music with the visual. The erosion of the presence of dynamic cultural forms in mainstream, prime-time TV means though that those matter-out-of-place moments seem less likely to happen. I am sure they will still occur, probably very rarely, but the conditions are not really conducive. This is reflective of the broader fragmentation of media. We can pursue our own interests and be immersed in the visual dynamics of music cultures in ways that just weren't previously possible, the question is whether those sudden jolting moments of movements clashing are still possible. Are such clashes of cultural streams still possible in mainstream TV? This also points to the underlying way that decentralised media can potentially keep ideas and cultural forms separate from one another. Yet, because people are consuming in their own different ways, if these moments do occur they might be more pronounced and carry even more power than the time that Nirvana momentarily infiltrated the prime-time talk show scene.

PLATFORM NOSTALGIA

The above presents some questions about how we might relate to the past and how that past might be presented to us in different forms. The collective past of TV game shows – with the increasing media savviness of participants today – or the subcultural moments of those past matter-out-of-place TV moments. Yet there is also a crucial change that these platforms bring that reshapes how we can literally view that past, whatever form it might take. The way we engage with the past, how we access it, is shifting in different ways. Social media give us a range of new vantage points for seeing that past.

Earlier this year I searched for a song from my youth – a pastime I imagine many of us engage in. I thought I might see if there was a live performance. An hour later I was listening to my second full These Animal Men gig. My original search had located the song I was after, but the recommendation algorithms hooked me in. One of the gigs suggested to me was a performance that had taken a place a week after I had actually seen the band in the summer of 1995. The rabbit hole led from that realisation; there were plenty of warrens to explore. I got sucked into a journey through time. Even for this relatively cult band, I found shaky camcorder videos of whole sets, TV appearances in various countries, interviews and other unseen footage. All of which, despite being a fan, I had never seen. I could revisit that period in a depth of material that far exceeded what I knew of the band back then. The lack of material at the time meant that bands were much more mysterious and enigmatic – I bought my first These Animal Men CD without really knowing what was on it. I was stuck in a particularly sticky form of nostalgia – it was immersive, detailed and hard to abandon. Indeed, these archives of popular culture have been described as 'affective archives' that are defined by the response we have to the content and the labour that people have put into creating and organising them.[93]

Social media have been with us for over a decade now. Their archival properties, which I described in my book *Popular Culture and New Media*, mean that they have shifted from being solely about networking and communication to a space for remembering our lives. Social media's capacity for revisiting goes well beyond the stories told by our profile updates. The sheer volume of materials means that almost any time, space, event, subculture or social movement can be revisited from any number of perspectives. The content stretches back beyond the 10-year period of social media and smartphones. Even the obscure can often be rendered available for revisiting. This has made possible a kind of *platform nostalgia* – where people upload as well as consume images, film and stories from past moments. There is a collective and shared nostalgia in these spaces – as well as what Mike Featherstone has described as an 'impulse' to archive[94] – driving people to share and contribute as well as immerse themselves in this past content. There are vast collections of materials and the stats often show high numbers of plays. These are crowd sourced audio, visual and textual histories, with people turning old videos into YouTube content and sharing observations and memories below the line. Social media have created new ways to access, discover or rediscover the past and to provoke our nostalgia. The past is brought closer to us in social media's archives, making it searchable and retrievable in a way that wasn't possible before.

It has been commented that we are living in a backwards focussed retro culture with a thirst for revisiting. Simon Reynolds, for example, has written of a new type of culturally defined 'retromania'.[95] Perhaps this tendency towards nostalgia has always been there but it is being unblocked and given new resources by social media – although others have found that these 'affective archives',[96] as discussed above, are more about the emotional attachments and commitments to the value of music that people have. The number of bands and artists that have got themselves back on the road is striking. From All Saints and Bananarama to The Stone Roses and Jamiroquai, this is a time for comebacks. As well as being a product of commercial interests these comebacks are rooted in the strong attachments that we forge with the music of our youths.[97] Perhaps the comeback is also a product of this platform nostalgia, with the music of the past now being much closer and much more available than before. The rise of platform nostalgia over the last decade may have paved the way and fuelled the sentiments that make these comebacks viable. This could be why the moment of the comeback has coincided with the era of social media (I will return to these comebacks in a moment).

We tend to think of social media as being distinctly contemporary, of the moment, as well as defining of our future. Yet they also give us a high vantage point from which to look backwards. As a social archive they are making individual and collective histories visible and accessible. The result is that the past has a stronger and more tangible presence. On this point, we can turn to two types of comeback: one an object and the other a movement.

ARE CASSETTE TAPES REALLY MAKING A COMEBACK TOO?

In the words of LL Cool J, don't call it a comeback. Yet quite a bit has been made of the increase in tape sales in 2018. The jump in sales is quite big, standing at 125%. On the surface it sounds like an acceleration in sales that replicates the recent resurgence of vinyl. But is tape really seeing a revival? If we look more closely, it seems more likely that something else is happening.

If we are honest, tapes were never a great way to listen to music. They gave us access to music, but they are unlikely to be anyone's preferred way of listening. We might have nostalgia for the time that we used tapes or for the music we listened to on the format, but people are unlikely to be that nostalgic about the format itself. They lacked the warmth and feel of vinyl, they lacked the quality and ease of skipping of a CD. The tape trapped you into linear listening, having to follow the tape from start to finish and back again. With tape it was hard to skip between tracks or to go straight to a particular song (this admittedly had some benefits, it made you listen to tracks that you might otherwise jump over). They were easily damaged and the quality wasn't always great.

Despite the drawbacks, tapes still had their value. They were more mobile than other formats of the time, they could be listened to on the move and stored more easily, and they were often cheaper than CD and vinyl. The best thing about tape was how easy they were to record onto. Purchased albums could easily be copied and mixtapes were a great way to share music.

Tapes also have a couple of advantages over streaming and download, which might explain the modest sales numbers of recent years – and why some bands and artists are choosing to release their music on cassette. Tapes have an actual material presence. They can be held, looked at, felt, displayed. The move from more material formats to streaming and downloads does lack this, it lacks the tactile material relationship that formats like tape provide – which might also be why people are turning back to vinyl.

For some, tapes carry a kind of connection with past experiences. They are an example of what Sherry Turkle calls 'evocative objects', they are objects that capture bits of our biographies. Some of the tape sales will be a product of people recalling the magic of buying music on tape and the excitement that went with it – especially when they were part of early musical experiences.

If we look more closely at the official sales figures,[98] they show that of the 50,000 tapes that were sold 7,523 were of The 1975's album *A Brief Inquiry into Online Relationships* and 6,262 were of Kylie Minogue's album *Golden*, both were limited edition (the Prodigy were third highest with 2,148 tape copies of their album *No Tourists*). So these two artists made up about a third of all the tapes sold in the year. This suggests not that people are going back to tape, but that certain limited or collector-type issues of tapes will do well and will boost the overall numbers. It seems that the tape is making a comeback not so much as a way of listening to music, although people undoubtedly are doing this, but more often as a collectable.

A few years ago tape looked like a dead format. Tape players weren't manufactured on the same scale and few artists and labels released material on the format. The increase in tapes is part of a return to a more material connection with culture that goes with increases in book and vinyl sales (although CD sales are still dropping). Sometimes people like to hold their music in their hands and put it, and their identity, on display in their homes. We can't think of tape sales increases as being a big change in itself. Fewer than 50,000 sales is modest, especially compared to 91 billion streams in the same year. The limitations of tape are likely to prevent people returning to it in large numbers, but it seems that cassettes still have a place in the complex mix of music listening practices we have today. What this small increase does suggest is that sometimes people like to have something tangible that represents their tastes, something that they can hold onto. Not all comebacks are quite what they seem, some are more significant than others.

THE RISE OF THE COMEBACK

So, what of musical comebacks? The announcement that 1980s pop trio Bananarama were to reform[99] represented just the latest in a long line of recent comebacks. From Boyzone to Wet Wet Wet, Take That to Jamiroquai, The Spice Girls, The Stone Roses, The Verve, Sleeper, S Club 7, 5ive and Cast, the list continues, musicians of the cultural past are taking advantage of an apparent wave of nostalgia. Even Menswe@r tried it, albeit with only one original member. The news that Elastica were reuniting,[100] however, disappointingly turned out to be premature – and revealed how a misunderstanding, in this case about the remastering of an old record, can be contorted and magnified into fact in social media spaces.

Comebacks seem to be everywhere. They are not limited to a particular genre, but they do often seem to be bound to a particular era. The success levels might vary somewhat, but we seem to be living in a cultural moment that is defined by the comeback. Of course, there have been plenty of comebacks before, but right now they are close to being ubiquitous. It's tricky to know exactly what is happening here. Music cultures have always had one foot in the past. Classic songs, signature sounds, attachments to older formats like vinyl, intertextual reference points, remastered and reissued albums and the like, have long been a central part of how music is made and consumed. But the comeback is a more material and pronounced version of these tendencies. The comeback represents a more obvious and direct impulse to revisit.

Nostalgia undoubtedly plays a part. Inevitably bands who return for a second innings are driven by a desire to revisit particular moments or to experience the music from more youthful times again. The myths and memories are likely to mix together a little here. Some suggest that the prominence of the comeback is further evidence of culture stalling[101]; that we have reached something of a creative dead end[102] and therefore can only look backwards.[103] The point here, mistakenly, would be to think that an absence of creativity has left a void that the comeback fills. A slightly more positive take on this is that we have seen the emergence, over the last 10 years or so, of a new kind of retro culture[104] which looks to the past for its resources and which uses pastiche to enliven culture today. This again could return us to what Simon Reynolds has called this revisiting of music's archive 'retromania'.[105] This may play a part, but I would suggest that we need look at alternative explanations that move beyond the halting or retro leanings of the music industry for the more recent rise of the comeback. We can gain a richer understanding of these comebacks by thinking about how music scenes are deeply rooted in individual identities – and about the important role that music takes in shaping how we connect with the social world.[106]

Research has shown, such as that by Andy Bennett,[107] that music fans continue to have an attachment to the music of their youth as they move into later life.[108] They might listen to other things and change their style of dress, but the music remains embedded in their identities.[109] We have a strong connection with the music that forms a central part of our own biographies.

Elsewhere it has been found that music plays an important role in how we handle our emotional lives. A classic study by Tia DeNora found that we use music in everyday life to influence and stimulate emotions and feelings, to negotiate moods or to help to recall or revisit memories and times.[110] This shows that people are likely to seek out opportunities to engage with that musical past both in terms of reaffirming their identities but also because of the emotions and memories that the music embodies for them. So we need not see these comebacks as a sign of cultural failure. This comeback music will have been central to how generations of people have negotiated their lives, so having a chance to experience it in the live arena is likely to be appealing. Music scenes, are, after all, moments when personal biographies mix with broader social changes and cultural movements.

The comeback is hard to explain because those explanations are likely to be based upon a kind of inbuilt nostalgia. When we compare music's past with its present we are also comparing different moments in our own lives. It is hard to understand changing music cultures when we are basing this understanding on our own changing biographies.

Yet Bananarama's comeback is undoubtedly part of a cultural movement, a comeback culture that is far greater than before. Like vintage and retro clothing, the resurgence of vinyl,[111] retro arcade video gaming, the trend for revisiting and remaking classic films and TV shows, and 'Keep calm and carry on' style memorabilia,[112] the comeback trend illustrates how complex relations are between yesterday and today.

The comeback is, above all else, fuelled by a desire to access and experience the cultural moments that defined individual lives and identities, not the collapse of cultural creativity. It is rooted in the attachments that people form as they live with music and as they recall those times and experiences. And so the political and social uncertainty that has defined recent years might well provide the backdrop for the comeback to thrive. It is much more likely that people are seeking assurance and security by turning back to the songs that provide an anchor for their identities or which enable them to negotiate the emotional impact of a seemingly uncertain social world, than that they feel alienated or disappointed by the music of today. The broader question that this chapter has so far suggested concerns the way that the media forms we now live with are intervening and shaping memory and remembering. We can also think more directly of social media as memory devices.

SOCIAL MEDIA AND MEMORIES

Social media has changed. Following more than a decade of popular use, the information in our Facebook, Instagram or Twitter profiles is no longer just about the current moment or instant connections. Instead of simply broadcasting our thoughts and actions as they happen, these platforms have become a biographical archive[113] of our lives, storing our photos and recording where we went and who we were with. The result of this archiving is that social media is taking on a new role in the way that we remember.

Even the most ephemeral social media platform, Snapchat, has now joined in this archiving process with the launch of its Memories feature in 2016.[114] Before that point, Snapchat's unique selling point has been that its picture messages were designed to disappear within seconds of being sent. This additional function allows users to build a 'personal collection of your favourite moments' (i.e. archive images taken with your phone), which can then be kept private or shared.

As I have mentioned, Mike Featherstone has argued that humans have a powerful 'impulse' to archive.[115] We even see this in the history of the modern state, which sought to capture and record[116] large amounts of information about peoples' lives. Smartphones and the internet mean that we can now satisfy this drive at the level of our everyday lives. Snapchat's Memories feature seems to exactly fit with this impulse.

So if we rely more and more on social media to archive our memories, how will it shape how we remember? As time passes, more of people's lives will be captured in these profiles. And when we want to remember our lives and the lives of the people we connect with, we will inevitably turn to the data stored in these social media archives. Our memories might then be shaped by the types of things that we choose to include in our visible social media profiles, or even in less visible spaces protected by our privacy settings[117] (as included in the Memories feature).

Featherstone has also argued that an archive, as a space in which documents are captured and classified, is 'a place for creating and reworking memory'.[118] What we put in our social profiles and how we classify it will then shape what is remembered and how those memories are recalled. For example, the tags and labels we add to photos stored online will affect what we later recall about the occasion and the people who were there. Of course, our social media profiles are filtered versions of our lives[119] that display a managed persona,[120] so they are likely to create an archive of certain types of favourable memories that fit with this persona.

As we come increasingly to rely on social media as an archive, the way we add to it will also inevitably change. We won't just be posting in the moment but will also have an eye on the future. We will be thinking about the way that our content will be received and will imagine how it will be drawn upon to remember our past from some unknown future moment. We might, for instance, post about our holidays on the basis of how we will wish to look back on that trip. It will change how we use social media to record any moment or period in our lives.

This is one of the ways in which the philosopher Jacques Derrida claimed that archives operate. He said archives are a kind of 'pledge' to the future.[121] We make judgements, he claimed, about what to include and how to tag it, based on how we imagine it will be used in the future. So, as people use Snapchat Memories and other services like it, they will be posting based on a vision of how it might be used in the future to evoke memories.

This use of social media to remember, with our profiles being individual and collective archives of our lives, will mean that the content created will shape future memories. These memories will be created and reworked through the choices we make about what to include in our profiles and will also be a product of how we imagine that memorialisation to play out in the future. Social media might be about broadcasting our lives and connecting with networks, but these new features mean that they are also based upon a pledge to future memories.

CONCLUSION

This chapter has briefly outlined how some of the quirks of contemporary culture illustrate how media are intervening in the relations between the past, the present and the future. Questions of nostalgia, comebacks and the mediation of memory are just some of the ways that these relations are being redrawn, almost without us noticing. Through these instances little insights can be found into these broader changes. With the archival form that decentralised media and platforms take, it is hard to avoid the conclusion that we are experiencing a changing relationship with the past. Something like total recall means that the act of remembering is distributed across humans and networked devices. Memory is something we can tap into rather than retain. As with the rise of data mining, platform culture presents us with a new politics of remembering and forgetting. These technologies are prosthetising memories, offering opportunities to bring the past much more directly into the present. The memory devices of the past, from souvenirs to photo albums, have been renewed. Beyond this, memory is a space of sharing in social media. Individual and collective memories circulate and are captured in various media archives (and categorised in the ways discussed in Chapter 2). Technologies are appending our memories and playing with them. These technologies are remembering more and also changing how we remember. It is not that this cultural recall is a problem in itself, although there is a politics of remembering and forgetting that it poses, it is that media platforms now play a much more direct part in shaping cultural relations with the past and with the future.

4

THE COMFORTS AND DISCOMFORTS OF CONNECTION

As culture moves onto platforms and as devices and interfaces embed themselves in our bodily routines, new types of tensions emerge. Connections bring with them a mix of comforts and discomforts, both reassuring us in some cases whilst taking on a disconcerting presence in others. In an essay from the early twentieth century, the sociologist Georg Simmel suggested that the presence of bridges and doors in the landscape revealed two human tendencies. On the one hand the bridge captures the 'will to connect', whilst on the other hand the door embodies the 'will to separate'.[122] Put simply, we have built material features into our landscape, embodied in bridges and doors, that enable these competing tendencies. A century or more later, bridges and doors remain as materialisations of these competing tendencies, and have been joined by a range of devices that both connect us and disconnect us. Perhaps the smartphone is a material form that combines these tendencies today. Phones enable us to connect, there is a comfort to be being contactable, but there can always be the disturbance, the unwanted connection that brings discomfort. Indeed, the smartphone is much more of a bridge than it is a door, it suggests that the impulse to connect has become dominant and shutting of far more difficult. Smartphones can still operate as doors, they can be shutdown, switched off or used to curb notifications and set privacy limits, yet they are somehow more porous and transparent as a social shield than the door. The will to separate is likely to remain, but the architectures we live in mean that it is more difficult to find the enclosures in which to exercise our will to separate.

As I will explore in this chapter, connecting and disconnecting relate closely to feelings of comfort and discomfort. From smartphones to social media, new connections bring with them a blend of comfort and discomfort, sometimes even creating a mix or tensions between the two. Consider that rare day when you forget your phone, the comfort it brings is lost but the disconnection can be liberating. On the other hand, think of how connections on social media can bring support but also feel disconcerting. We have a complex weaving of comfort and discomfort that comes as we become connected into platform cultures of different types.

THE COMFORT OF A SMARTPHONE

A little while ago I made the mistake of putting my mobile phone in the washing machine. Despite being quickly retrieved, the phone died. I left it to dry out for a few days, but nothing. There was an encouraging flashing light, but this was a false dawn. Breaking your phone is probably a fairly common experience and shouldn't be too much of a problem (the sight of someone swiping over a cracked screen is commonplace), but what I was surprised about was the feeling that it created. There was something disorientating and unsettling about not having my phone with me. This moment of stupidity was a moment of rupture for my normal routines. It provided me with some insight into just how much we rely on mobile devices. This reliance is not just based on the fact that these phones allow us to keep in touch, to stay networked and to participate in the incessant din of social media. The response I had was not just about the missing functions of the phone and my sudden inability to stay networked. Rather this was about the comforting presence that these objects have in our lives.

We might go as far as to say that we develop something of an emotional attachment with our smartphones, particularly as they become embedded in our bodily routines. They provide a comforting weight in our hands, pockets and bags. We slide them out, check them, hold them and place them back. When we think about the impact of phones, we usually just think about what it is that they can do. But they also have a material presence in our lives. Our relationship with them is tactile and physical. They are not just devices or portals onto an informational world, they are also objects.

As I mentioned when reflecting on the apparent comeback of the cassette tape, Sherry Turkle has used the phrase 'evocative objects' to think about the types of connections that we have with the things that we surround ourselves with.[123] Turkle's point is that what seem like quite mundane objects can have profound personal meanings for us – triggering memories and emotional responses. For Turkle, we should think of these types of evocative objects 'as companions to our emotional lives or as provocations of thought'.[124] We connect to these objects and use them to negotiate and stimulate emotional responses or to trigger thoughts and feelings. We share experiences, moments and sentiments with these objects – which, in Turkle's edited volume, can range from a camera, to a suitcase, to a rolling pin and to a yellow raincoat. This is what the anthropologist Daniel Miller has called the 'comfort of things'.[125] His study of a street of 30 households revealed a deep connection that the residents had to the stuff that filled their homes, these objects were seen to have a comforting presence in their lives. We probably all have objects around with which we have a strong emotional attachment, and which are both evocative and comforting. I am sitting writing this next to a miner's lamp which I keep on my desk, it means nothing to anyone except me. Yet, for me, it brings both strong memories and a sense of familiarity and reassurance.

In the 1930s, Walter Benjamin wrote some brief reflections on what it was like to be reunited with his book collection – it had been in transit when he had been forced to move across Europe.[126] Benjamin uses that experience of prizing open the packing cases to reflect on the attachment that he had with his books. His essay explores the importance of the materiality of the book collection. Benjamin's book collector sees through the objects into their past. Part of our attachment with these objects, Benjamin's piece suggests, comes from the shared biographies of the book and its owner – the yellowed paper, the coffee stains, the dog eared pages and the dusty cover. He suggests that what is written in the book is not necessarily the only thing that is of importance to the collector, rather it is the presence of that book in the glass case or on the shelf that matters – the cloth, cardboard, paper and binding that can be held in the hand or put on display. Benjamin's attachment to his books is material. It is not about the function of the media, but their presence in the collector's life.

As we live with them, we develop a kind of personal attachment with our phones. This is so familiar to us now that we might only notice it in moments of rupture –when a phone is lost. We might even go as far as to say

that they are 'evocative objects' with which we have a visceral bodily connection. Although we move onto the next phone when the time comes for an
upgrade, transferring this temporary attachment to the next phone – perhaps
experiencing a brief moment of uncertainty and discomfort in these moments
of change and before our new object becomes familiar. We are attached to
what it is that these devices can do, facilitating our creeping connectivity, but
they are also objects that are comforting and reassuring.

It could be argued that smart devices have a kind of comforting effect. My
experience with my broken phone suggests that they are not only reassuring
us in this way, but that they are also comforting in their material presence
as objects in our lives and in our hands. It is perhaps hard to separate these
mobile media devices themselves from their functionality, but it does help us to
notice how attached we have become to their presence. Smartphones, it seems,
are comforting both in the functional role that they perform and as potentially
evocative objects that are, as Turkle put it, companions to our emotional lives.
This forces us to ask what other comforts such devices might afford.

BODIES IN BUBBLES

In the 1980s one of the defining images of cool, for me and my friends at
least, was Michael J. Fox skateboarding away from school whilst listening to his Walkman in the classic 1985 film *Back to the Future*. The Huey
Lewis and the News soundtrack might sound a little bit dated today, but
what has become much more established and widespread is the practice of
listening to music (or other audio content) whilst on the move. The year
1985 was relatively early days in the history of mobile music, but now such
practices are much more ordinary and familiar. It is not hard to see how
important mobile devices of different sorts – and earphones – have become
in people's lives.

Millions of these devices have been sold around the world, following
the tape and CD Walkman the iPod took the market share but has now
been usurped by the convergence of technologies in the smartphone. Even
just glancing around as we move through any public space we see people
holding their devices and earphones plugged into ears. There have been
arguments made about this representing the end of social space, that people are withdrawing from social contact and that these devices are illustrative of the individualisation processes that are a defining part of the
modern world.

There might well be some merit in these arguments. Certainly it would seem that escaping into this alternative soundtrack is at least allowing that person to tune out from their surroundings. In these arguments listening to music whilst mobile becomes a kind of social shield. This social shield is then used to cut out unwanted interaction, noise and to lift that individual out of the discomforts of their surroundings.

Indeed, the few social scientists who have written in this area tend to write of the mobile music device as being, to use Marshall McLuhan's terminology, a kind of 'earlid' that can cut out the overwhelming cacophony and din of our everyday worlds.[127] The argument tends to be that these mobile music devices can be used to reclaim public territory in order to make it private and controllable, and that mobile music devices provide us with a means of shutting out the oppressive downward forces of the urban metropolis as it impinges upon our senses. Mobile music devices can be imagined as being a tool for protecting the bodily and sensory territory against the backdrop of the unrelenting spaces of modernity, and can cut us off from the more uncomfortable moments we experience.

Similarly, these mobile devices are depicted as a means for enchanting the more humdrum spaces through which we pass, a means of bringing to life familiar places and routines, of soundtracking spaces with interesting and evocative music that stimulates our memories and emotions. Indeed, Michael Bull, the most prominent of the social scientists working in this area, describes mobile music devices as providing us with a means of controlling, managing and negotiating the experience of everyday life.

We can see then that the popular vision of mobile devices is that they are extremely powerful in their reshaping of ordinary day-to-day experiences. But is this stretching things a bit? Are these devices really this powerful? Are they really able to cut us off from sensory experiences and social connections? When we reflect this does seem quite extreme. As an alternative, I have argued previously, we could instead think of these devices as providing us with moments within which we are able to 'tune out'.[128] That is to say that they provide us with temporary moments of distraction, but that we still experience the noise around us, the environment we are in and maybe we even still find ourselves in unwanted social interactions. The place we are in is still able to supersede the mobile music, to make it difficult to hear, to force is to remove the earplugs and to hear what is being said, and so on.

The difficulty is that it is quite hard to think outside of the idea that we are living in times of individualisation, a time in which we are witnessing the ongoing collapse of social bonds. As a result, we tend to see these devices in the same terms. When we think about their undoubted influence on people's lives and the places we inhabit, it becomes hard to see them in any other way. In this sphere of thinking it has become common to imagine mobile music devices as creating a sonic 'bubble' around us. This is a vision of a cultural shield that cuts out various sensory and social encounters in favour of a more enjoyable and less chaotic set of experiences. In this vision of the mobile music device as bubble, we have a visual metaphor for social withdrawal. If we apply this bubble idea to our streets, towns, cities and even homes, we would begin to imagine public spaces as being populated by bodies within bubbles: each individual moving independently within their own enchanted little 'enclave',[129] both occupying the space whilst being cut-off and separate. We might even expand this vision beyond mobile music to imagine that something similar might be happening through the use of mobile devices in general.

It is tempting then to fit mobile music consumption into what have been described as the broader cultural trends of withdrawal, isolation and segregation. These bubbles could be seen to be part of the same processes that are responsible for people shutting themselves away in gated communities, fortifying their homes, gentrifying neighbourhoods, using VIP lounges, driving door to door in armoured cars and so on. In other words, the bubble image in mobile music, and the vision of people using these devices to shut themselves off from their surroundings, forces us to think about the way they feel about other people, about strangers and about the world they occupy. These devices are being imagined, essentially, as temporary zones of exclusion or segregation driven by a sense of discomfort.

In his book *Bubbles* Peter Sloterdijk has argued that in the modern age we are shell-less, a condition, he argues, that has been brought about by the collapse of some of old certainties.[130] As a result, Sloterdijk claims, we look to create shells or bubbles around ourselves. In these bubbles, we can find a new sense of security. Through the shared image of the bubble we might begin to see mobile devices in these terms, with Sloterdijk's vision of shell-less insecure people looking for some sense of bubble-like security. Mobile cultural consumption then becomes not just a social shield; this concept of the bubble also urges us to think about how something like music consumption speaks to these broader issues of withdrawal, fear and insecurity.

The problem is that I am not sure that anybody really knows just how integrated these devices are in social withdrawal. These devices can of course be a source of social interaction and identification. But perhaps the main problem is the one I have already alluded to, these devices are not as powerful as we might be imagining. The immediacy of our surroundings cannot be escaped all that easily, we might merely be prioritising the music and tuning out the other things we are experiencing. If mobile music devices are creating bubbles of culture around us then we might need to remind ourselves that bubbles are fragile, they can be popped. They might offer us a means of enchanting space but they lack the solid boundaries of other forms of more material segregation, such as those occurring in cities. Perhaps then the bubble is a good metaphor because it allows us to see mobile music as a means of escape or momentary security that is easily open to interruption or invasion by our surroundings.

The bubble metaphor might be helpful in imagining the way that listening to music on the move works, but we need to be careful that we don't see these as concrete sonic bubbles that are simply ending our connections with our immediate environment. Bodies in technology-afforded bubbles, the 'mediated skins' as Sloterdijk referred to them, might have become a normal sight in the years since Michael J. Fox's skateboard school run, but the images and narratives we draw upon to understand mobile music tend to overplay the power of the devices for shutting out social and material interactions with the world around us, and they also tend to overlook the way that these devices are part of a wider infrastructure of cultural participation, networking and consumption.

THE COMFORTS AND DISCOMFORTS OF SMARTNESS

I used to see smartness as tyrannical. This was over 15 years ago, when I was toiling away in a cold-calling telephone sales job. I tried to communicate my struggles to my manager. I was working hard, I informed him, but with little success. His response was simply to point out that I should 'work smarter, not harder'. The message, as I interpreted it, was simple: failure is your fault – the product of your lack of ingenuity, limited initiative and absence of guile. You are not entrepreneurial enough. You are not smart. The blame lay squarely on my shoulders. Smartness made my inadequacies tangible. I wasn't competing effectively. This was one of those 'brushes with neoliberalism on a granular scale' recently described by the

writer Philip Mirowski – moments when we discover that 'competition is
a primary virtue, and solidarity a sign of weakness'.[131] Smartness was the
vehicle by which the individualising properties of contemporary capitalism
found their way into my life. I was jolted into these memories by a gift
from a supermarket – a complimentary bottle of Smartwater that came
with a supermarket food delivery. Smartwater, we are told, is inspired by
'nature' and 'clouds' and includes 'electrolytes'.[132] The implicit suggestion
is that this is water that adapts to our individual needs for hydration. This
appears to be a new product, but it's not the first time I have come across a
mention of smartwater. A few years ago I was at York railway station and
noticed a large billboard informing me that 'smartwater' was used in the
city – in this case to stain the clothes of criminals and make them visible to
law enforcement officers.

So today, smartness is still a means for promoting individualisation,
but it finds its way into our lives in the very objects that surround us.
Such notions of smartness are now ubiquitous, like the advert for smart
toothpaste that recently appeared on my TV.[133] This is a kind of toothpaste
that knows your mouth better than you do. It can change its actions to suit
the needs of your breath, plaque levels, cavity prevention, enamel erosion,
whiteness and so on. It judges these needs for itself, with autonomy and
thinking-power, treating us as individuals.

The most obvious presence of smartness in our lives is in our phones.
Smartphones have been a mainstream presence since around 2007, when
the iPhone was launched, and over the last 10 years they have become
familiar and established their presence. Smartphones have become a part
of bodily routines, narratives and lifestyle images, and are deeply woven
into the social fabric. They are a part of how people live. Their smartness
is celebrated and enthused over. Smartphones learn about us in different
ways and respond to our needs. They predict things about us and what we
might want to know. We get recommendations through them. We get noti-
fied. We get anticipated.

The idea of smart objects is a notion that can be placed at the boundary
between technology and science fiction, a line that is often blurred. Encour-
aged by science fiction, designers have been imagining smart technologies
for many years, like the smart fridge. This is a fridge that notes which items
of food are getting low and orders replacements. It is likely to be found
in the kitchen of a 'thinking home'[134] that adapts to how you live and
guesses what temperature, humidity or light levels you would like without

you asking.[135] Radio frequency identity tags are often used in these types of technologies – minute sensors that can be embedded in objects, spaces or bodies to give them a unique identity code that can be scanned. These tags lead us to envision the 'internet of things' and the enmeshing of the material and immaterial. The connected environment is seen as the smart environment.

These environments are already with us, but in a more humdrum form. We have on-demand TV and music streaming services that predict our tastes, and make recommendations. Indeed, recommendations are everywhere and are delivered to us by lots of smart devices. These aren't the only things they are used to predict, it has even been claimed that music streaming data can be used to infer consumer confidence for making economic predictions.[136] With these platforms, culture and capitalism are never far apart.

In her cyborg manifesto, which is now over 30 years old, Donna Haraway anticipated that as devices become more mobile and bodies are technologically enhanced, people will become increasingly cybernetic[137] – connected with each other and with machines in systems of communication. Cyborgs and cybernetic imagery are often used to explore the blurring lines between humans and technology. The result, for Haraway, is that human beings will become directly connected into their surroundings. Her conclusion was that people will become 'frighteningly inert', whilst the technologies they live with will become 'disturbingly lively'. The cyborg metaphor was frequently used in the 1990s and 2000s to evoke both the passive body and the energetic technology that connects people with their informational environments.[138] So the underlying consequence of smart objects, this might lead us to believe, could be passive and sedentary human beings.

However, as smartness has become a leitmotif of modern life, notions of liveliness and passivity have become more complex. Rather than people simply becoming immobilised by machines, smart technologies might be seen to assist in the training of the self or as thoughtful facilitators of self-improvement. Smart technologies make our homes supportive of our lifestyles and future-proof our bodies by making them fitter, cleaner and more efficient.

In some cases, they do the work for us, and with devices like Fitbit or applications like Strava – which track and compare fitness and lifestyle data – there are cases where smart technology is pushing the body towards *heightened* activity, though still based on individualised competition and the use of metrics in search of the 'perfect lifestyle'.

Pierre Dardot and Christian Laval have argued that 'practical exercises in self-transformation tend to transfer the whole burden of complexity and competition exclusively onto the individual'.[139] Smart objects play the dual role of training what might then be thought of as a neoliberal subject whilst also allowing people to feel that they have some help and assistance with the individualised burdens and complexities of contemporary life. They stretch us, but they also make us feel that we are more able to cope with the pressures that are placed upon us.

There is something comforting about the idea that the objects that surround us are smart. We are made to feel special by these objects. They give us personalised service. They know about us – intimately. This promotes feelings of a life lived in an environment in which all our needs are catered for.

These objects also enhance our own sense of smartness. They make us feel as though we do indeed work 'smarter, but not harder', and perhaps they even know things about us that we don't know ourselves – like the type of dental issues diagnosed by my smart toothpaste. The object is the expert, so we can trust them to know what to do. They are thoughtful, autonomous, and deeply individualising.

But tucked away in these notions of smartness is also the 'everyday neoliberalism' to which Mirowski has referred.[140] They contribute towards our effectiveness as self-trained, individualised, entrepreneurial subjects, whilst also offering the comforting reassurance that they are taking care of us. Smartness as a concept and set of devices brings ideals that potentially incorporate these broader political dynamics into our everyday lives. Smartness also brings with it a blend of comfort and discomfort.

SOCIAL MEDIA'S COLLECTIVE BACKFIRING

In his recent book *Nervous States* the political economist William Davies argues that our times have been defined by a long-term weakening of the binaries 'between mind and body, and between war and peace'.[141] The changes in these binary distinctions are central to the anxious and nervous states that he explores. Some of my earlier discussions might be understood in relation to the former, but let us now reflect on the latter. In describing the weakening of the boundary between war and peace what emerges in Davies' panoramic account is that we are now experiencing, as he puts it, 'conflict intruding into everyday life'. Of course, conflict has always had a presence in everyday life, Davies' point is that its presence is far more defining and constant. Central to this rising conflict is a shift in the forms of media we consume.

In the last couple of years the concept of the 'filter bubble', developed by Eli Pariser back in 2011, suddenly seemed quite urgent.[142] I probably don't need to say why, but the escalation of concern over misinformation and the sudden need to understand how social media facilitate the spread of news caused the concept to draw lots of attention. Its frequent use meant that it even became a cliché of sorts. In contrast to this popular vision of how social media limits our window on the world, Jamie Bartlett – responding to an article by Brenden Nyhan and Jason Reifler[143] – used a short piece to explore why the 'backfire effect' might be, in his view, a better way for understanding the damage that has been done to political debate and the conflictual nature of these social media interactions.[144]

In this case, the 'backfire effect' is used to describe how our encounters with opposing views actually reinforce our own existing views – rarely are people persuaded to change their minds by ideas or arguments that run counter to their established notions. Bartlett's intervention neatly describes how this concept can be used to understand social media interactions. One key point he makes is that rather than simply filtering out alternative points of view, social media constantly present us with views that frustrate, annoy or anger us.

It's an important observation. We commonly see people voicing such emotions. In the week that I read Bartlett's piece I don't think I was aware that Andrew Adonis was even on Twitter. Following some bizarre comments he made about academics' summer holidays and his subsequent goading of the academic community, I repeatedly saw a handful of his tweets as people, understandably riled, shared and responded to the comments. I suspect that no one's views of what academics do was changed much by these exchanges. It seems more likely to have entrenched existing views on both sides. That's just one example of what, I think, Bartlett is pointing towards. You won't need to look far to find lots of others.

Having said this, Bartlett's vision might be overlooking (or at least understating) the collective way that this 'backfire effect' often works. It seems to have a kind of community forming property. This might be negative, with collective adherence to damaging or prejudicial views becoming harder to challenge. Reductive and populist ideas might find purchase by creating accounts of the world to act against rather than persuade otherwise. Yet, in the case of Adonis' comments, a good deal of solidarity was expressed within the outrage. People shared their frustration as they shared comments. It might be that social media are based around the connection forming properties of 'the backfire effect' that Bartlett refers to – as well as the individual cementing of views that it is said to cause.

This can happen algorithmically as well as being a product of how social media are used. Algorithms are unlikely to hide counterintuitive content from us, they like things that stimulate activity of any sort. The 'backfire effect' is one way that activity can be provoked. But it is also significant as a phenomenon because of the way social media are used.

The sociologists Imogen Tyler and Bruce Bennett have discussed how certain celebrities act as 'bad objects'.[145] As people distance themselves from those celebrities, they share in that act of distancing. The bad object becomes a symbol that people can collectively differentiate themselves from. So, the bad object enables social connections to be forged and maintained – whilst also perpetuating various social divisions and patterns of abjection. We could see the content that enables this shared backfiring as being bad objects – with people connecting by acting together to distance themselves from that content. Collective backfiring.

Rather than representing a totally different way of understanding social media, the backfire effect can even contribute to the filter bubble. When these alternative perspectives or narratives arrive they are shared within a network and are often explicitly identified as some sort of illustration of what is seen to be wrong, what shouldn't be and what falls outside the accepted positions of that network.

When we see 'backfire' type content – that is, stuff that we don't like or agree with or which goes against our logic, but which ultimately solidifies our existing views – it often comes with commentary from other social media users that contextualises our potential disdain and cements its 'backfire' credentials.

We don't necessarily need to reject the idea of the 'filter bubble' to explore this backfire effect. The filter bubble doesn't mean that we only see things we agree with or see as rational, it means we see things that support our world view. These could be things we feel are wrong but which we and others are using to create the boundaries of our bubbles and give our social networks inward coherence. This includes things that we despise, feel we know to be wrong or which we think are misleading. It's just that these things are deployed within networks to distance and create boundaries and norms. It might be that the backfire effect is part of how the filter bubble operates and how social media reifies perspectives. It might not be, as Bartlett argues, the 'reverse' of a filter bubble or echo chamber.

Either way, the shift here is in thinking of the power of a kind of collective backfire effect, rather than seeing it as an entirely individual response. Culture and the public sphere is full of such backfiring, and so the connections these media bring also stir up issues and facilitate, and maybe even exacerbate, conflict, distrust and division.

THE DISCOMFORTING POWER OF OUR SOCIAL MEDIA DATA

The collective backfiring described above brings discomfort to the connections and interactions we have with others, behind those interactions, of course, the infrastructures are drawing upon our data to try to direct actions, behaviours and connections. The power of the crew-neck capitalist, as I briefly outlined in the opening chapter of the book, is not something we should be taking lightly. More than this though, the type of power dynamics shouldn't necessarily be understood or accepted in the terms that they are usually described to us. The stories about Cambridge Analytica and the use of Facebook data swept across the media in 2018.[146] Perhaps the most striking were the stories of dramatic headquarter raids.[147] An accompanying TV expose left an impression of these skulking figures lurking in the shadows, seeking to use our data to control us.[148] The idea that we can be manipulated via our data is, admittedly, very concerning and a little intimidating. This is a type of power, informed by our data, that acts upon us in surreptitious ways, shaping our worlds below the level of our consciousness. At least, that is how it might seem.

Of course, companies like Cambridge Analytica have a reason to promote such visions of the power they wield through data. They seek to inflate the value of the data, their main asset, by talking-up its potential. As a result, the lens through which we are now seeing the power of data is at least partly built by them and by this industry. Cambridge Analytica were an unusual case, they are quite different to most other data analytics providers. This inflation of the possibilities was part of their attempt, it would seem, to cultivate a shadowy fixer type image.[149] By emphasising the idea that our data can be used to get inside our heads, what are referred to as 'psychographics' are part of the image that is being cultivated.[150] Such ideas are undoubtedly built upon a fairly crude logic, a logic that is based upon the premise that *we are our data* and therefore our data can be used to remake us. This is not to say that such use of data in things like political messaging and targeting has no power, far from it, we just shouldn't approach these questions by accepting the type of visions that these figures project upon themselves and their use of our data.

Cambridge Analytica and others within data analytics seem to be trying to exercise two types of power. The first type is based upon this use of people's data to shape or tailor the world that individuals encounter in their social media feeds. Part curation and part manipulation, they try to know us though our data. It seems likely that it is at least possible to cement or amplify certain world views by targeting ideas at those already receptive to them. We shouldn't accept this power uncritically, but we should also resist the temptation to reject it out of hand for its implied ideas about people's inability to resist and reject. Simply accepting or outright rejecting the power that can be exercised through our data doesn't really get us very far. Even if people aren't so easily manipulated as we might be led to believe, which they aren't, the use of data targeting is still shaping what is known and might still be setting the terms of the debate. Dictating what people encounter will inevitably have effects, but just not necessarily those that are being suggested (such as the ability to swing an election).

This leads us to the second type of power, which is based on the way that these data and their possibilities are imagined. Part of the power being exercised here is located in the type of visions of an all-seeing and all-knowing politics that are being carefully built.[151] This type of vision is bundled up in notions of psychographics and how, through their voluminous data resources, analytics can change individual's views and behaviours. These things may not be achievable in the ways being suggested, but there is a power in this set of imagined capabilities. Such powerful visions of data are persuasive and create opportunities for data-led thinking and approaches to spread and dominate. The aim, it seems, is to project a kind of authority upon those using these types of data analytics, that authority then lends them political capital.

In terms of the broader context, 'Platform Capitalism'[152] is, of course, as I have discussed, underpinned by the value of our data. Targeting people using their data is not the exception, it is the whole point. It is targeting that enables data to be turned into value. Facebook's value is based largely upon its data. The fact that these news stories undermine the potential future use of data may well be why Facebook was reported to have lost

$60bn within a few days of those news stories breaking.[153] Of course, the data alone have little value. As mentioned, the value of data is actually in its imagined potential. In other words, the value of our data is in how it might come to be analysed, what it might be used to infer about us, how it might be used to predict or promote certain actions, behaviours, tastes and choices. With the potential of data located in its future value, the imagined possibilities are ever more important, especially as they come to mix with the realities.

In the abstract, we probably all know that this data harvesting is going on, but what seems to jar is when the realities of these processes are made clear and tangible to us. This might be why the Cambridge Analytica stories gained such attention – we instinctively knew this was going on but the materiality of the stories suddenly made it real. The realities have suddenly clashed with what we imagined. This is where the problems of consent have revealed themselves to us and where we are presented with an opportunity to reflect more directly on how power is being exercised on us through our own data.

When it comes to the value of social media companies, the key thing to remember is that it is you, the user, that has created that value. You are the worker. The key assets are the data produced through profiles and interactions. We are engaging in what has been referred to as 'free labour' but on a mass scale.[154] All of this poses the question of why we continue to work so hard and so diligently for social media companies so that they can both create value out of us and then use the fruits of our labour to try to manipulate us. Over the last couple of years many have been reflecting on how we might change things.[155] So powerful is the decade long imposition of social media in everyday life that an alternative is hard to imagine. There are a lot of things that are far easier to imagine than a life without social media. It seems unlikely that people will suddenly be horrified enough by these various events, or whatever versions of these events that are yet to come, to delete their Facebook accounts, social media are simply too embedded in how people live and relate to one another.

By way of a solution, some have called for escalating regulation of the sector, this would be welcome but it will be hard to manage on a transnational scale. These platforms span the globe and are part of a complex geographical media ecology – though this certainly shouldn't stop us trying. One of the more radical ideas is to nationalise Facebook (and,

potentially, other social media platforms) or create nationalised alterna-
tives.[156]. An issue here might be the problem of state ownership of such
data – it also asks the question of where such platforms would be nationalised. Paul Mason has explored some of the options, suggesting that
we might both break-up and nationalise Facebook at the same time.[157]
There have also been calls to use antitrust laws to break up the big tech
platforms[158] – although these firms are now building their own stock of
anti-trust expertise.[159] Taking a slightly different line, one option might be
to turn Facebook, and possibly other large scale social media platforms,
into a mutual. It would then be owned by its workers, by which I mean
ordinary social media users, allowing its benefits and profits to be shared
collectively. The profits could then be used for global and collective developments and initiatives. This, effectively, would be to think of social media
as part of a mutually owned commons.[160] As well as creating revenues for
collective projects, such a shift in ownership would change the motiva-
tions behind the use of the data – it would be free from the imperative
to manipulate in order to make ever greater profits. We could then have
a different type of platform whilst also changing the way data are used,
thought of and deployed.

Solving this situation will require changes in the way our data are treated, it will also need us to shift how we think of the labour that produces
those data in the first place. The alternative is to continue down the path
that we have been on for quite some years, a path that leads to ever more
data harvesting and ever more profound attempts to fold that data back
into our lives. I would suggest that we think much more structurally and
reflect not just on the data of the individual but on the whole purpose and
ownership of these collective spaces.

THE IDEALS AND TENSIONS OF OUR SOCIAL MEDIA SPACES

Visibly nervous, striking a repentant pose, on the 10 April 2018 Mark
Zuckerberg faced several hours of questions at a joint hearing of the Sen-
ate's Commerce and Judiciary Committee.[161] The early days of April 2018
proved to be a long couple of weeks for the Chairman and CEO of Facebook. Gone was the trademark T-shirt. In its place, a more formal collar and tie. The shift in attire seemed to fit with the controlled contrition
on display. The casualness of the crew-neck capitalist was absent, for the
moment at least.

As might have been expected, the discussion was of regulation, transparency, consent, consumer choice, election interference and privacy protection. In all of this, a key exchange was about chocolate. Mr Nelson, a ranking member, recounted how he had been interacting with someone about his favourite chocolate, afterwards he found himself confronted with lots of adverts for chocolate. There was a naïveté to the exchange that exposed the soft underbelly of government and the limited knowledge of the platforms, yet the question somehow cut to the heart of things. What if I don't want to get personalised targeted adverts, he asked. It's a familiar experience, but the question forced Zuckerberg to discuss the Facebook business model in rudimentary terms. His answer indicated that people don't mind adverts if they are relevant to them – so by targeting us with content they are actually helping us to have a better experience. An advert supported service is the only way for Facebook to work as a free service, he later responded. Zuckerberg was also asked how he can sustain a business model where people don't pay. His answer was simple, 'Senator, we run ads'. The smiling bluntness of the answer was revealing. It was reiterated in another exchange, with the observation that advertisers tell them who they want to reach and they help them to do that. These various scattered moments laid bare, in very stark terms, Facebook's business model.

In the written testimony[162] submitted in advance of the hearing, much of which was reiterated in the discussions, Zuckerberg claimed, boldly, that Facebook is an 'idealistic' and 'optimistic' company. This was echoed in the hearing. These ideals underpin both what Zuckerberg thinks went wrong and the solutions he is proposing. But what are these ideals? And what is the model of the world that informs this optimism? These ideals seem to be based on the idea that data can solve our problems, that we should be evermore connected into our networks, that our media experiences should be increasingly tailored and that platforms empower and offer voice. The same visions can be flipped to take on much more dystopic properties of inescapable media and the integration of a kind of constant and ongoing data-led nudging of us towards certain desired outcomes. The problem here is that the ideals and optimism are based upon a vision that is not necessarily shared by everyone, yet there seems an unshakable confidence that we all want the future that they are imagining. If we want to challenge this we don't just need more regulation, we need to challenge the very ideas and principles that guide and justify how our data are being used.

As this hearing made painfully clear, using data to target and shape behaviours is an integral part of social media. It is the potential use of our data that is of real value. Data informed targeting is woven into social media's DNA; the only way to change that is to change their structure and purpose. Under questioning Zuckerberg suggested that Facebook is going through a 'broader philosophical shift', taking them from simply producing tools for 'empowering' people to the need now to take a 'more proactive role' in 'policing the ecosystem'. This implies that they seek an even more powerful position – both as producers and regulators – and a larger role-out of their particular ideals and philosophies.

The answer to the problems of Facebook, it seemed to be suggested, is more Facebook and more of its current business model. The account was of a purer Facebook that gives you connectivity, voice and control of your information, untainted by any issues, missteps or unwanted players. An enhanced version of what we already have is what was being proposed as the solution. Putting the obvious problems to one side for the moment, the other question is whether we really share the ideals of Facebook. The tone of this hearing was apologetic, but it leaves us to question if change is actually possible. We might trust Zuckerberg and his 'team', whom he repeatedly referred to, to be responsible, this doesn't mean that we need to accept the ideals that are wrapped up in these media and the type of world that is being imagined. The problems clearly need attention, but we might also wonder about the ideals that will play such a powerful part in our collective future. The ideals and models of Facebook will continue to expand unless we think a little more about the future that we want to bring into existence.

THE COMFORTS AND DISCOMFORTS OF BEING WATCHED AND LISTENED TO …

It is almost not worth saying that media technologies have significantly expanded the reach of surveillance in the last decade or so. It is fairly obvious. This surveillance has been well covered and is a striking feature of the devices and media forms that are now embedded into the textures of everyday life. The ideas of a 'surveillance society' are never far away.[163] If we put the more obvious instances to one side, we can perhaps find something else about the directionality of the gaze of surveillance, especially if we think in terms of watching and being watched. Platform culture is highly visual. We watch. We are watched. We see. We are seen. This visual set of relations forms into feedback loops. The things we watch are watched, which is then used to feed into the things we watch and so on. Something like TV is not a one-way flow of information, it's another opportunity to gather data and to make us visible – and then we have the responses to those TV shows which then circulate in hashtags and other social media content. Alongside this, platform culture creates new possibilities for seeing and watching, as well as increasing the variety of things over which we might cast an eye. Wherever we look we are being asked to watch and often in return we are then watched ourselves. Attention becomes a key commodity in consumption and in surveillance. Platform culture is defined by the act of watching. In platform-based digital cultures we glance quickly in lots of different directions, and we are also looked at from different vantage points. Unpicking all this is almost impossible. Given the complexity of all this watching, the difficulty is knowing where to start.

THE TV CALLS YOUR NAME

In 2017, whilst using an on-demand service to catch up with one of the many shifting political debates, I was caught off guard by a 'personalised' TV advert. This was not something I had seen before. The advert for Ronseal Fence Life began by saying my name to me. As far as I could tell it was only personalised insofar as it opened by addressing me directly, it wasn't, for instance, personalised enough to know that I don't own a fence.

It turns out that Channel 4, the channel I was watching at the time, introduced what it calls 'the world's first audio personalised TV ads' on the 25 April 2017.[164] Developed by the media company Innovid, the three partners for this launch were Fosters, 20th Century Fox and Ronseal. Quoted in the press release, James Smith, Ronseal's Marketing Director, suggested that 'this new technology provides us with the ideal platform to get personal so we can motivate people to finally get on with their DIY'.

A bit of motivation is always welcome. It would seem though that the change in the adverts is more directly connected to the possibilities for capturing our attention. David Amodio, Channel 4's 'Digital and Creative Leader', indicated in the same press statement that:

> the most attention grabbing word for anyone to hear is, without doubt, one's own name, so to be able to offer advertisers the chance to speak directly to our millions of viewers is not just unique, but an immensely powerful marketing tool.[165]

It seems that calling out someone's name is seen to represent an opportunity to monopolise attention. It's almost as if someone in advertising has got hold of Louis Althusser's essay 'Ideology and the Ideological State Apparatus'[166] that I discussed in Chapter 1. As I mentioned in Chapter 1, in that essay Althusser uses the metaphor of being hailed in the street to explain his concept of 'interpellation'. When hailed we can't help but look, he points out, in that moment we are exposed to culture and its embedded ideologies. These ideologies call to us all the time. Althusser was pointing to what he saw as the inescapability of being subsumed into ideologies, whether we choose to resist or not. There is a kind of gravitational pull to being hailed.

In the case of these personalised TV adverts we have a kind of consumerist hailing going on. It seems that the aim of using the viewer's name, drawn from their account details, is to try to make it impossible for you not to look. This change is presented, with the adverts opening 'personalised advert' message, as being about shaping content to the needs of the user. It is in keeping with the type of faux-familiarity discussed earlier, and is accompanied by the emphasis on convenience and the tailoring of experience that we saw in the rhetoric of the crew-neck capitalist. It's obvious though that this is not really about personalisation, it's about hailing. It's about shouting at us to catch our attention.

As Althusser pointed out, when shouted at it is hard not to turn and glance. Saying your name is a more powerful way of grabbing your attention than simply including it as text. The problem is that this now adds to the cacophony of hailing that comes at us incessantly. It's like they are testing to see if sonic hailing is a way to be heard over the rest of the calls for our attention. Sound cuts through, plus our name is an attention-grabbing audio signal.

The problem is the feeling that this personalisation produces. It got my attention but it felt like a stranger saying my name at me, producing a feeling of uneasiness rather than providing any warm sense of a knowing dialogue. By being addressed, I felt like I was being watched. These personalised TV adverts have the desperation of Alan Partridge, in a car park, repeatedly shouting 'Dan' to try to get the attention of what he hopes is his new best friend.

This type of faux intimacy is quite common. These can be placed within the broader 'cold intimacies' of capitalism described by Eva Illouz[167] – hollow gestures that suggest a caring presence. We are returned to the over familiarity of the crew-neck capitalist. This pretence of being friendly and of knowing us is a well-worn tool of capitalism. Birthday and Christmas cards and messages from brands and corporations, recommendations and suggestions sent to us with personalised messages and a familiar tone. There are lots of ways that, as Will Davies has described, 'technology has put itself on first name terms' with us.[168]

Sound is not only now at the forefront of surveillance, with questions about how microphones embedded in phones and voice-activated consumables generate sonic data; it is also being used within the attention economy. Listening without speaking in the former case and speaking without listening in the latter. There is a kind of inescapability to being hailed by your name.

The tailoring of the soundscape is not to cater to our needs it is to call our attention, to hail us in a way that can't easily be ignored or that cuts through the information bombarding us. In the pursuit of attention, which is a rare commodity within the context of what, as we have seen, the media theorist Mark Andrejevic has called the 'infoglut',[169] sound is being used to create new opportunities to limit our spaces of escape and to channel our focus towards desired objects. As I will go on to discuss, this adds a sonic dimension to this 'infoglut'.

The danger is that our soundscapes become as cluttered with attempts to grab our attention as our visual lines of sight already are. This will give us even less space or peace in which to escape, think and reflect. Returning us to the image discussed in Chapter 1, imagine what it will be like if our media start constantly saying our name to us, hailing us in lots of directions, repeatedly calling for our attention.

THE SOUND OF SURVEILLANCE

The 1974 film *The Conversation* leaves us with the image of an increasingly fraught surveillance expert trying to work out how he is being spied upon. Frazzled by paranoia he strips his apartment bare. The fixtures, fittings and even some of the plaster from the walls are removed in a desperate attempt to extract any secreted bugs or devices. The undiscovered and unsuspected source, as is suggested in a tech-fair featured earlier in the film, is his telephone – the microphone of which can be turned on even when the receiver is in place. The ageing pro is being destabilised by the new surveillance tech. This new surveillance is based on existing and embedded technologies rather than added bugs or cameras, making it much harder to detect or remove.

The Conversation suggests a concern with the impending power of audio surveillance. The outcome it points towards is a future of inescapable ears and an associated rising paranoia. When we think about surveillance today we often think about the importance of data, which we imagine as binary code of 0s and 1s, or as text, numbers and visual images – photos, film, data visualisations and the like. We think of the new surveillance powers in visual terms. The panopticon is our reference point for thinking of a world in which we can always be seen.[170] But seeing is not the limit of the data extraction today, it is also in the hearing.

The 40-year-old visions provided in *The Conversation* no longer seem particularly intimidating. The reason for this is simple. We now seem comfortable with surveillance technologies being embedded in our lives, most of the time they go unnoticed or we give them little thought. Surveillance is part of consumption; it is presented as the pay-off for the promises of convenience that crew-neck capitalism bases itself upon. *The Conversation* seems quaint in comparison to recent accounts of the call centre, to pick out an example of a particularly data rich workspace. We now have a vast assemblage of technologies capturing our work, leisure, consumption and even bodily routines. The seeing is escalating, but so too is the hearing. In fact, it seems it is the audio data that is now starting to boom in a way that couldn't easily have been envisioned.

It would seem that the forces associated with a predictive and automated capitalism are driving sonic data harvesting, which is then used to develop a more rounded and detailed knowledge of our lives (or, as we saw earlier, to call for our attention). This knowledge can be used to tailor, target, predict and promote. The soundscape is now trackable in ways that previously were not possible. The audio properties of social space can now be interfaced with networked technologies. Soundscapes can be transferred into data, meaning it can be treated like and combined with other data.

Most obviously we have the listening powers of ubiquitous smartphones. The social world is now packed with microphones. People are also wondering if their phone's microphones might mean that tech companies, hackers or even the state might be listening to them, a paranoia is perhaps building.[171] Reports that social media companies might be listening using the microphones on smartphones caused some reaction and also some debate about exactly what the microphones are used to do.[172] The suggestion was that installed apps might be used to listen for targeted advertising opportunities, based on background music or TV and the like. It's a feature that can be turned off, but it is the possibility of being listened to by the apps that have access to our microphones that is important here. This gives a sense of the scale of potential sonic data extraction and of the pervasive listening infrastructures in which we now live.

It is not just that companies might potentially now be listening to us that is important, but it is the general shift towards a sense that this is a useful and even desirable way in which to engage with consumers that is crucial. It suggests the underlying logic that is gaining traction. In the summer of 2017 there were reports that the BBC was partnering with Microsoft to test a new feature for iPlayer that would allow it to listen to the voices in the room.[173] Once it had discerned who was in the room it would tailor the content and recommendations accordingly. It is not clear if these plans will ever materialise, but the underpinning pursuit of sonic surveillance for the stated purposes of personalisation is clear. The idea that people want to be listened to by their devices is striking here.

In addition, we also have devices like the Amazon Echo. These are beginning to obtain significant sales momentum, with the suggestion the home has never before been exposed to such a level of 'corporate surveillance',[174] they also point to a future of audio activated devices in the home. Recent media coverage has been asking what these devices hear and what is extracted. A 2017 episode of the TV show *The Good Fight* featured a fictional automated and voice controlled 'Ada' device being seized so that an inadvertent recording could be used in court.[175] This storyline suggests that these ideas about the possibilities of sonic surveillance are bubbling in the popular imagination. In reality, these various sonically controlled devices only start listening when their keyword is used, but they are still listening out for that keyword. It's not clear exactly what audio is captured. A recent court case involving an Echo may reveal some of what is extracted, if the data are made available as evidence, but this remains unclear.[176] What is clear is that the voice controlled devices are opening up new questions about the ethics and scale of sonic surveillance in automated consumer services. The sense that we might be listened to is starting to build. There have been claims, for instance, whether founded or not, that these types of devices can accidentally be triggered (in one reported case a device inadvertently captured a conversation that was then sent to a friend[177]). Despite the protestations that the devices don't listen to us, the reports of the patenting of 'voice-sniffing' technology,[178] which listens out for different types of advertising trigger words in conversations, or that Facebook have patented a system that enables 'your phone mic to monitor TV habits'[179] do little to ease the concerns. It is the growing sense that we might be listened to that is as important here.

To point to just one other illustrative example, the workplace is also rapidly becoming a site of data led sonic surveillance. The new worker badges that listen to interactions provide an example of the networking of the sonic spaces of the workplace.[180]. These badges listen out for the tone of voice in customer interactions and the like.[181] These possibilities for sonic analytics expand as part of broader trends in workplace tracking.[182] The increasing presence of networked devices in our lives has vastly increased the opportunities for harvesting data. But the new frontier in data extraction is based upon the ability of these active devices to listen to us. We are seeing a vast expansion of a new kind of sonic surveillance.

The film *The Conversation* may now seem dated, limiting its ability to provoke our fear of surveillance. The home-space[183] and workplace[184] have now been networked for some time, we are used to it. Plus, its vision pales into almost insignificance when we reflect on how the whole of the social world is now embedded with microphones. As convergence led to a far greater presence of cameras, so too the embedding of phones has led to digital and networked microphones being everywhere. Despite these changes, the 1974 film does still suggest something. It suggests that when we are confronted with bemusing listening environments we, like the surveillance expert, may end up frazzled with paranoia and unable to find and strip these embedded bugs from our everyday lives. The desperate efforts of Gene Hackman scrabbling to find out the source of his leak may be an image that somehow captures a future in which sonic data become the new frontier in data-based surveillance and tracking. This is not necessarily about whether we are actually being listened to, it is the sense or possibility that we might. Like the surveillance expert, our paranoia of a sonic panopticon is the issue. It is the possibility of sonic surveillance that is important.

CONCLUSION

The experience of culture today is often a site of tension and mixed emotion. Comfort is one way to think of this, but focussing on comfort alone is a limiting in what it can tell us. Connecting into networks brings possibilities that can be tempered by a range of new problems and uncertainties. I have not explored it in this chapter, but something like privacy brings with it all sorts of uncertainties that can be discomforting in all sorts of ways. Yesterday I was searching for trainers on the Adidas online shop, after leaving the site without a purchase I received an email asking if I needed help finding something. The disconcerting sense of the surveillance of consumer capitalism is never far away, even if we have trained ourselves to feel comfortable with it. On a very simple level, privacy was fairly routinely demarcated in the near past, a reasonably clear line could be drawn between the public and the private. The private was relatively impermeable beyond things like gossip. Instead now social media users are constantly having to make decisions about where this line should be drawn. Decisions about the level of sharing are constant and inescapable for social media users. There is a comfort that comes from sharing, but a discomfort that might be brought about were we to overshare or to reveal something outside of the kinds of norms, rules and etiquette that has emerged. Such decisions are now routine, but are nevertheless a source of potential tension. In short, there is a tension between comfort and discomfort in these digital cultures. I have touched upon some of the sources of such tension in this chapter, but there are many more to explore.

Outside of these experiences, the above has reflected upon how power can be a source of discomfort with networks. So, within these networks there is both the possibility of access and empowerment, whilst there is also the problem of power acting upon us through networks and algorithms. This chapter shows the tensions of connectivity and disconnectivity occurring in digital culture. Platform-based cultures are a site of tensions, as culture has always been, but these tensions seem to play out in the comfort and discomfort of the limits of experience on the one hand and the problems of empowerment and disempowerment on the other. This chapter begins to illustrate how on-demand culture – including its devices and platforms – place us in this tension between comfort and discomfort. These two feelings blend together in digital culture and define what it is like to engage with culture on platforms. The possibilities and reassurances are nearly always tempered by at least a background or fleeting sense of unease. The promises of convenience and perfectible social connections mean that the unease and discomfort are often written off as an acceptable pay-off.

5

THE DEMANDS OF
ON-DEMAND CULTURE

It's late June 2018, I turn over a magazine to be confronted by a full back-page advert from Facebook.[185] 'Fake news is not our friend' it reads. The rest of the advert, in a brief flourish, tells us that they are committed to reducing the spread of fake news and that they are using more fact-checkers to improve the reliability of content. This is platform culture: an age when social media companies feel the need to tell us that they will seek to deliver us only the truth. The campaign, in various forms, seemed to last for the rest of the year and is continuing as I complete this book. Full-page adverts in various publications emphasising, in broad terms, that we can trust Facebook to do the right thing. Repeatedly telling us that they share our values and want the same things as us – as I have discussed in this book, the visions are important here but so is the reach of social media into people's lives and even across the mainstream press. Where inadequacies, leaks and a lack of control over the data are exposed, which has happened in a series of events, they race, very publicly, to resolve them.[186] This isn't just about Facebook – there are some early indications that the social media tastes of younger people might lie elsewhere[187] and a recent Pew Research Center report indicated that Facebook is now only the fourth favourite social media platform amongst US teens[188] – but it is indicative of a way of thinking, an approach that permeates across the media landscape. What this does suggest is that the social media ecology is likely to change, and its demands and ethos may also alter over time. What is continuing to escalate in a more uniform way is their reach and the depth of embeddedness in people's lives.[189]

Writing around 1915, the sociologist Georg Simmel observed that:

> the vast intensive and extensive growth of our technology ... entangles us in a web of means, and means toward means, more and more intermediate stages, causing us to lose sight of our real ultimate ends.[190]

These reflections on the role of technology, in what he referred to as the *crisis of culture,* were, of course, a response to very different political times, yet the sentiment of this passage echoes on. Our technological systems have increased in intensity, moving deeper into our lives, whilst spreading outwards into networks. Our media push inwards whilst reaching out. The result, for Simmel, is that we are entangled in these systems, they add layer upon layer, making it hard to separate out the means from the ends. His point is that amongst all these layered technologies and fragments of information we actually lose sight of our sense of purpose. In short, the problem modernity brings is that we get so caught up in what we can do, so distracted by the layers of tasks, interactions and processes, that it becomes hard to maintain a sense of direction or focus.

Few writers had a better grasp of the gathering forces of modernity than Simmel. David Frisby went as far as to describe him as the 'first sociologist of modernity'.[191] Simmel who died in 1918, wrote on varied topics, from fashion and food to city life and secret societies, but he always had an eye on the unfolding consequences of modernity. With sensitivity to those early shifts, his writings carry a sense of the direction things were heading.

Simmel had long been interested in how modern life was changing everyday experiences. In a piece from the early 1900s he reflected on what these changes meant for the senses. His conclusion was that we end up becoming 'short-sensed', meaning that we feel things up close ever more intensely whilst feeling distant from the wider world. We simply can't cope with the sensory overload brought by the unfathomable information and the many experiential stimuli, so we focus more intently on the immediate. With modernity, life was taking on an increasingly 'fragmentary character', he later argued. The more fragments we are faced with, he claimed in his later works, the more we are able to assemble the bits to suit and reinforce our conception of the world – our conception of the world gives a frame for those fragments, which in turn, over time, shape that frame.[192] In a wide-ranging and thoughtful piece on the changing relations between technology and democracy, Jamie Bartlett points out that the ability to find examples that we can curate or compile to support our views is a bigger issue than the so-called 'fake news'.[193] This ability to manoeuvre the fragments in support of an idealised or particular world-view was something Simmel observed and began to conceptualise. The greater the range of fragments the greater the possibilities for cementing those perspectives, and also the greater the possibility for people to assemble very different world views from the shards of information.[194] If this is the case, then we can imagine how, with our current personalised, on-demand and algorithmic media, the fragmentary character of life Simmel was observing will have escalated along with the possibilities for world making. Not only are there far more fragments, the way we encounter those fragments has changed in recent years.

Nick Srnicek has argued that as platforms

> reach out further and further into our digital infrastructure and as society becomes increasingly reliant upon them, it is crucial that we understand how they function and what can be done.[195]

Not least, we might wonder what happens to culture and to our cultural experiences when they are moved onto platforms. We may not necessarily get to fully grasp the platforms themselves, but that does not mean that we are unable to see the engrained changes they bring to our lives and the possible futures that they are easing us towards. Part of imagining what can be done is understanding how the platforms reshape culture and the way we relate to it. Srnicek also argues that 'how we conceptualise the past and the future is important for how we think strategically and develop political tactics to transform society today'.[196] There is a sense that the shifts in these technologies present us with questions about what future we want to bring into existence and, along with that, bring into play the politics of those visions. In this book, I have offered only a brief intervention, yet the point I hope to make from it is that by finding the quirks and unusual aspects within culture we can begin to understand and potentially have more of a say in the directions that culture takes in the future. Seeing behind the slick exterior to locate the features and direction of culture might present opportunities to challenge and resist or simply to acknowledge and make choices. I argued in Chapter 3 that the relations between the past, present and future are changing in interesting and sometimes compelling ways, and it is that relation with the future where most might be gained.

As I explored in the opening chapter, a kind of crew-neck capitalism forms the background context to the cultural formations described. We now face the demands of our on-demand culture. I started the book with reference to Althusser's concept of interpellation and hailing, suggesting that hailing is now a screaming street scene of competing voices calling to get us to look. We don't know which way to look first or what to respond to. Interpellation is a fragmentary experience. We can't possibly look in all the directions from which the calls emanate, so we have partial encounters with culture, encounters that suit us and that are based on who happens to shout the loudest at us. The loudest shouts are those closest up. They achieve this proximity through the kind of algorithmic sorting of content and through the personalisation of our media spaces. As a result, on-demand or platform culture requires a different understanding of how we are absorbed into cultural relations, our role within them and what we get from them. There is a new type of tension in the fragmentation and prioritisation, a dynamism and flux that replicates the past but hypes it up to unprecedented levels. Culture and media are working in new types of relations that both define everyday experience whilst making it much more difficult to grasp.

Naturally, we tend to focus on what an on-demand culture can deliver to us at our convenience, we might also reflect on what it demands of us as well as what we demand of it. The demands of on-demand culture are just as important. They tell us about the pay-off of convenience and accessibility. When the shift in culture is from ownership to access,[197] the power dynamics reconvene around those points of access. I have touched on the dynamics of these points of access in the previous chapters of this book. These points of contact are transforming our relations with culture, and they are also at the same time changing the cultural forms themselves. These recombinant intersections between cultural forms and cultural consumption continue to unfold. In short, moving culture on to the platform does not just change how we relate and consume culture, it also reshapes the culture itself.

In terms of the transformation of the relations and experiences of culture, I have explored here some of the ways in which our relations with the past are reconfigured, I also looked at the tensions between comfort and discomfort that these cultural relations bring. Before that I looked at the new types of cultural ordering processes that underpin these shifts. This is only a brief book, a piece of 'sociological impressionism',[199] that is intended to introduce a series of ideas and openings, it offers momentary and fleeting insights into some of these shifts. My hope is that it will rip at some of those fissures so that they can be explored or used, perhaps, to question and examine what platforms mean for the way we relate to culture and the cultural forms themselves. The nature of these changes is so deep and varied that capturing it in its entirety seems almost impossible. Its unfathomability and scale are part of its distinctive properties and are a defining part of what is going on. My approach in this short intervention was to try to find some little quirks that give us a glimpse below the surface of these cultural relations. If we look carefully, there are lots of these quirks – they just often pass unnoticed in the large part. Maybe we can pause on those strange oddities or these little ruptures and use them as opportunities to see what is unfolding on a broader scale. This is to use these moments to disrupt norms and dominant ideas within the vast flows of contemporary culture. These are the hooks on which we can hang our thinking even as we get swept along by these swirling masses of content.

As the chapters have indicated, the decentralisation of culture is not necessarily causing its democratisation. Who is watching or listening to whom, how memories are shaped or interactions prioritised, how we discover things, how tastes are defined and so on. The spaces on these platforms are not flat or neutral. In some ways that terminology of the platform might be misleading, it encourages us to think of a flat, shiny and even surface on which transactions, interactions and consumption occurs. We know that they are quite different. Platforms of the type we are discussing here have a topology and are three dimensional – within and on them we find ourselves in hierarchical positions looking up, down and across at the content and protagonists that come into view. More like mountain ranges than ice rinks, once culture moves to the platform it becomes part of their uneven landscape.

Rather than open and democratic spaces we are looking instead at the new power structures and power concentrations that are afforded by platforms and an on-demand type cultural experience. Decentralisation does not mean the end of monopolies, there can be new concentrations of power.[199] A fragmentation of culture can cover for a narrowing of power.

Where culture is on platforms and takes this kind of on-demand form then attention and visibility become the focus. It is about drawing our attention in certain directions – where before it was about placing the cultural form in the spaces where most would already be looking or listening. Who gets heard is important, the hailing that gets a reaction is crucial. This is how power operates. What gains attention, what becomes visible, is a product of a careful working of the mediascape to certain advantages. This is not all negative, as the chapters have made clear, as well as bringing problems on-demand culture also brings new social connections, vast opportunities for eclectic cultural engagement and a dynamic and energised cultural sphere. I have tried to capture this most directly in the chapter on comfort and discomfort (see Chapter 4). There is a tension between the opportunities and richness that on-demand culture brings and the discomforts of conflictual interaction, unrelenting connection and data manipulation. On-demand culture brings choice but it also brings a sense of inescapability. Any account that reduces this only to the negative or positive implications will be overly simplistic and will miss the very tensions of comfort and discomfort that define these cultural shifts. The cultural experiences we have in the context of digital culture at once provide the means for access, eclecticism, insight and possibility, whilst also bringing the pay-off of surveillance, manipulation and a disconcerting sense of inescapability. The question this leaves unanswered is how platforms manage to maintain this combination of comfort and discomfort.

On-demand culture is forged in this tension. It brings cultural richness and access whenever it is desired, within certain limits, whilst also making demands of us in return. There is a new cultural vibrancy, an eclecticism, a new level of access, creativity and expression, but this sits in tension with the more uncomfortable, invasive and manipulative aspects that I have also discussed. Culture has always been a loose term that attempts to capture something almost unfathomable, but on-demand culture brings with it a vitality and variety that only exacerbates that existing problem. The problem is where to start when trying to grasp it. There are little glimpses behind the curtain that we can find if we look carefully for those little oddities and quirks. Most importantly, though, if we want to understand what is going on we should consider the demands that are made of us by our on-demand culture and the platforms that support it.

NOTES

1. Nick Srnicek, *Platform Capitalism*, Cambridge: Polity Press, 2017. See also Paul Langley & Andrew Leyshon, 'Platform capitalism: The intermediation and capitalisation of digital economic circulation', *Finance and Society* 3(1), 2016, 1–21.

2. Louis Althusser, *On the Reproduction of Capitalism*, London: Verso, 2014, 232–272.

3. Louis Althusser, 264 (Italics in the original).

4. Louis Althusser.

5. Louis Althusser.

6. Louis Althusser, 265.

7. Louis Althusser, 232–272.

8. I take this phrase from Georg Simmel, for a discussion see David Beer, *Georg Simmel's Concluding Thoughts: Worlds, Lives, Fragments*, London: Palgrave Macmillan, 2019.

9. David Beer, 'Making Friends with Jarvis Cocker', *Cultural Sociology* 2(2), 2008, 222–241.

10. As reported by Rhiannon Williams, 'More than friends: Facebook to set up dating service', *i newspaper*, 2 May 2018.

11. Aliya Ram, 'Apps gather a wealth of personal data', *Financial Times*, 24 October 2018.

12. Catherine Miller, Rachel Coldicutt & Hannah Kitcher, 'People, power and technology: The 2018 digital understanding report', Doteveryone, 2018, available at https://understanding.doteveryone.org.uk

13. First published in 1916, this essay was published in English translation as Georg Simmel, 'The fragmentary character of life', *Theory, Culture & Society* 29(7–8), 2012, 237–248.

14. David Frisby, *Sociological Impressionism: A Reassessment of Georg Simmel's Social Theory*, Second Edition, London: Routledge, 1992.

15. Nick Srnicek, *Platform Capitalism*, Cambridge: Polity Press, 2017.

16. Zygmunt Bauman, *Collateral Damage: Social Inequalities in a Global Age*, Cambridge: Polity Press, 2011.

17. Geoffrey Bowker & Susan Leigh Star, *Sorting Things Out: Classification and its Consequences*, Cambridge, Massachusetts: MIT Press, 1999.

18. For the announcement from Yell see https://business.yell.com/media-centre/yell-becomes-purely-digital-business-final-publication-yellow-pages/

19. The record can be found at http://www.guinnessworldrecords.com/world-records/most-telephone-directories-ripped-in-two-minutes-(spine)

20. Yell's YouTube channel containing these adverts is available at https://www.youtube.com/user/yell

21. Tarleton Gillespie, 'Algorithmically recognizable: Santorum's Google problem, and Google's Santorum problem', *Information, Communication & Society* 20(1), 2017, 63–80.

22. Geoffrey Bowker & Susan Leigh Star, *Sorting Things Out: Classification and its Consequences*, Cambridge, Massachusetts: MIT Press, 1999.

23. David Beer, 'Genre, boundary drawing and the classificatory imagination', *Cultural Sociology* 7(2), 2013, 145–160.

24. Michel Foucault, *The Order of Things*, London: Routledge, 2002.

25. Alex Hern, 'Facebook lets advertisers target users based on sensitive interests', *The Guardian*, 16 May 2018, https://www.theguardian.com/technology/2018/may/16/facebook-lets-advertisers-target-users-based-on-sensitive-interests

26. Theodor M. Porter, *Trust in Numbers: The Pursuit of Objectivity in Science and Public Life*, Princeton: Princeton University Press, 1995.

27. Ian Hacking, *The Taming of Chance*, Cambridge: Cambridge University Press, 1990.

28. Imogen Tyler, 'Classificatory struggles: Class, culture and inequality in neoliberal times', *The Sociological Review* 63(2), 2015, 493–511.

29. Kasia Narkowicz & Nisha Kappor, 'The character of citizenship: Denying the rights of asylum seekers and criminalising dissent', *Open Democracy*, 20 May 2017, https://www.opendemocracy.net/uk/kasia-narkowicz-nisha-kapoor/character-of-citizenship-denying-rights- of-asylum-seekers-and-crimin

30. See, for example, the BBC Newsbeat report from the 7 March 2018 https://www.bbc.co.uk/news/newsbeat-43318898

31. David Beer, 'The pop-pickers have picked decentralised media: the fall of Top of the Pops and the rise of the second media age', *Sociological Research Online* 11(3), 2006, http://www.socresonline.org.uk/11/3/beer.html

32. Adam Sherwin, 'NME axes 'unviable' print edition ending 66 years of rock music', *i newspaper*, 7 March 2018, https://inews.co.uk/culture/music/nme-axes-unviable-print-edition-ending-66-years-rock-history/

33. Mark Poster, *The Second Media Age*, Cambridge: Polity, 1995.

34. David Beer, *Popular Culture and New Media: The Politics of Circulation*, Basingstoke: Palgrave Macmillan, 2013.

35. The planning documents are available at https://planningdocuments.warwickdc.gov.uk/online-applications/applicationDetails.do?activeTab=summary&keyVal=_WARWI_DCAPR_71753

36. The planning committee minutes from the Town Council of Royal Leamington Spa meeting of the 3 December 2014 are available https://www.google.co.uk/url?sa=t&rct=j&q=&esrc=s&source=web&cd=1&ved=0ahUKEwipm-Od9cjRAhWlIsAKHZ8aAGUQFggdMAA&url=http%3A%2F%2Fleamingtonspatowncouncil.gov.uk%2Fcontrols%2FDownloadDocument.ashx%3FdocID%3Dcc2714VMZQTNHDUXWV8320iCwl%26aID%3D2484&usg=AFQjCNEa1gKYUWKzn584myx-hm9g5BkDCA&sig2=9dhlWebV-Pczgm6rsZvNSA&bvm=bv.144224172,d.bGg (accessed 17 January 2017)

37. Information about the Alveston Place development is available at
    http://www.alvestonplace.co.uk/

38. The Alveston Place sales brochure was available as an online sales
    brochure which has now been removed.

39. See the BBC report 'HMV calls in administrators for the second time
    in six years' https://www.bbc.co.uk/news/business-46699290

40. David Beer & Mark Taylor, 'The hidden dimensions of the musical
    field and the potential of the new social data', *Sociological Research
    Online*, 18(2), 2013, http://www.socresonline.org.uk/18/2/14.html

41. Rob Davies, 'What caused the pound's flash crash?', *The Guardian*,
    7 October 2016, https://www.theguardian.com/business/2016/oct/07/
    what-caused-pound-flash-crash-brexit-fallen-sterling

42. David Beer, 'The embedded power of algorithms', *Open Democracy*,
    3 July 2014, https://www.opendemocracy.net/david-beer/embedded-
    power-of-algorithms

43. George Dvorsky, "Rogue' Algorithm blames for historic crash of
    the British Pound', Gizmodo, 10 July 2016, https://gizmodo.com/
    rogue-algorithm-blamed-for-historic-crash-of-the-britis-1787523587

44. Jonathan Albright, 'Algorithms might be everywhere, but like us,
    they're deeply flawed', The Conversation, 19 October 2016, https://
    theconversation.com/algorithms-might-be-everywhere-but-like-us-
    theyre-deeply-flawed-66838

45. Stephen Graham & Simon Marvin, *Splintering Urbanism: Networked
    infrastructures, technological mobilities and the urban condition*,
    London: Routledge, 2001.

46. Frank Pasquale, *The Black Box Society: The secret algorithms that
    control money and information*, Harvard: Harvard University Press,
    2015.

47. Nigel Thrift, *Knowing Capitalism*, London: Sage, 2005.

48. Cathy O'Neil, 'How algorithms rule our working lives', *The Guardian*,
    1 September 2016, https://www.theguardian.com/science/2016/sep/01/
    how-algorithms-rule-our-working-lives

49. Leo Hickman, 'How algorithms rule the world', *The Guardian*,
    1 July 2013, https://www.theguardian.com/science/2013/jul/01/how-
    algorithms-rule-world-nsa

50. Leigh Alexander, 'Is an algorithm any less racist than a human?',
    The Guardian, 3 August 2016, https://www.theguardian.com/
    technology/2016/aug/03/algorithm-racist-human-employers-work

51. Cathy O'Neil, 'Big-data algorithms are manipulating us all', *Wired*,
    18 October 2016, https://www.wired.com/2016/10/big-data-algorithms-
    manipulating-us/

52. John Naughton, 'Machine learning: why we mustn't be slaves to the
    algorithm', *The Guardian*, 16 October 2016, https://www.theguardian.
    com/commentisfree/2016/oct/16/slaves-to-algorithm-machine-
    learning-hidden-bias

53. Louise Amoore, *The Politics of Possibility*, Durham: Duke University
    Press, 2015.

54. Taina Bucher, 'The algorithmic imaginary: exploring the ordinary
    affects of Facebook algorithms', *Information, Communication &
    Society* 20(1), 2017, 30–44.

55. David Beer, 'The social power of algorithms', *Information,
    Communication & Society* 20(1), 2017, 1–13.

56. William Davies, 'The age of post-truth politics', *The New York Times*,
    24 August 2016, https://www.nytimes.com/2016/08/24/opinion/
    campaign-stops/the-age-of-post-truth-politics.html?_r=1&referer=

57. Dave Lee, 'Facebook's fake news crisis', *BBC*, 15 November 2016,
    https://www.bbc.co.uk/news/technology-37983571

58. Hannah Jane Parkinson, 'Click and elect: how fake news helped
    Donald Trump win a real election', *The Guardian*, 14 November
    2016, https://www.theguardian.com/commentisfree/2016/nov/14/fake-
    news-donald-trump-election-alt-right-social-media-tech-companies

59. For a discussion of the transformation of news media over the last
    two decades see James Meek, 'The Club and the Mob', *London
    Review of Books* 40(23), 6 December 2018.

60. This has been widely discussed, see, for example, William Davies, 'The age of post-truth politics', *New York Times*, 24 August 2016.

61. For an introductory discussion of this concept see Eli Pariser, 'Bewar online "filter bubbles"', Ted2011, https://www.ted.com/talks/eli_ pariser_beware_online_filter_bubbles

62. Amelia Tait, 'How to burst your social media bubble', *New Statesman*, 11 November 2016, https://www.newstatesman.com/science-tech/ social-media/2016/11/how-burst-your-social-media-bubble

63. David W. Hill, "Total gating': Sociality and the fortification of networked spaces', *Mobilities* 7(1), 2012, 115–129.

64. Rowland Atkinson, 'Padding the bunker: Strategies of middle-class disaffiliation and colonisation in the city', *Urban Studies* 43(4), 2006, 819–832.

65. Rowland Atkinson, 'Fortress UK? Gated communities, the spatial revolt of the elites and time-space trajectories of segregation, *Housing Studies* 19(6), 2004, 875–892.

66. David Beer, 'Tune-out: Music, soundscapes and the urban mise-en-scene', *Information, Communication & Society* 10(6), 2007, 846–866.

67. Barry Wellman, Anabel Quan-Haase, Jeffrey Boase, Wenhong Chen, Keith Hampton, Isabel Diaz & Kakuko Miyata, 'The Social affordances of the Internet for networked individualism', *Journal of Computer-Mediated Communication* 8(3), 2003, https://doi.org/ 10.1111/j.1083-6101.2003.tb00216.x

68. David Beer, *Popular Culture and New Media: The Politics of Circulation*, Basingstoke: Palgrave Macmillan, 2013.

69. Sam Thielman, 'Facebook fires trending team, and algorithms without humans goes crazy', *The Guardian*, 29 August 2016, https://www. theguardian.com/technology/2016/aug/29/facebook-fires-trending-topics-team-algorithm

70. David Beer, 'The social power of algorithms', *Information, Communication & Society* 20(1), 2017, 1–13.

71. Ben Williamson, 'Algorithms in the news – Why digital media literacy matters', Code Acts in Education, 19 December 2016, https://codeactsineducation.wordpress.com/2016/12/19/algorithms-in-the-news/

72. Gabriel Pogrund, 'Post-truth v tech: Could machines help us call out politicians' and journalists' lies?, *New Statesman*, 17 August 2016, https://www.newstatesman.com/2016/08/post-truth-v-tech-could-machines-help-us-call-out-politicians-and-journalists-lies

73. Mark Andrejevic, *Infoglut: How too much information is changing the way we think and know*, London: Routledge, 2013.

74. Chris Foxx, 'Twitter axes Vine video service', *BBC*, 27 October 2016, https://www.bbc.co.uk/news/technology-37788052

75. For a discussion of the diffusion of memes see Jens Sieffert-Brockman, Trevor Diehl & Leonhard Dobusch, 'Memes as games: The evolution of a digital discourse online', *New Media & Society* 20(8), 2018, 2862–2879.

76. Madhumita Murgia & Hannah Kuchler, 'Twitter prunes vine and cuts workforce by 9%', *Financial Times*, 27 October 2016, https://www.ft.com/content/d4f32c86-9c3c-11e6-a6e4-8b8e77dd083a

77. Andrew Griffin, 'Twitter videos to become extra long as vine also drops six-second limit and lets people make huge videos', *Independent*, 21 June 2016, https://www.independent.co.uk/life-style/gadgets-and-tech/news/twitter-videos-to-become-extra-long-as-vine-also-drops-six-second-limit-a7093431.html

78. Judy Wajcman, *Pressed for Time*, Chicago: University of Chicago Press, 2015.

79. Mark Andrejevic, *Infoglut: How too much information is changing the way we think and know*, London: Routledge, 2013.

80. Dave Gorman, *Too Much Information*, London: Ebury, 2014.

81. Katherine Viner, 'How technology disrupted the truth', *The Guardian*, 12 July 2016, https://www.theguardian.com/media/2016/jul/12/how-technology-disrupted-the-truth

82. Scott Lash, *Intensive Culture: Social Theory, Religion & Contemporary Capitalism*, London: Sage, 2010.

83. This was also a position that Georg Simmel develops in his later works around the period 1914–1918 as discussed in David Beer, *Georg Simmel's Concluding Thoughts: Worlds, Lives, Fragments*, London: Palgrave Macmillan, 2019.

84. John Tomlinson, *The Culture of Speed: The Coming of Immediacy*, London: Sage, 2007.

85. Daniel Rosney, 'The year of the debut chart smash', *BBC Newsbeat*, 31 December 2014, http://www.bbc.co.uk/newsbeat/article/30642014/the-year-of-the-debut-chart-smash

86. Rupert Till, 'Streaming hits the top 40, but is this the end of the chart itself', The Conversation, 24 June 2014, https://theconversation.com/streaming-hits-the-top-40-but-is-this-the-end-of-the-chart-itself-28370

87. See the Official Charts list of 'All the Number 1 Singles', Official Charts, 8 March 2019, available at https://www.officialcharts.com/chart-news/all-the-number-1-singles__7931/

88. When I was working out these averages, where a song had dropped down the charts and then returned to number one, which tended to happen more in the early days of the charts, I only counted it once – as this is a return rather than a new chart topper.

89. Georg Simmel, 'The philosophy of fashion', in, David Frisby & Mike Featherstone (eds), *Simmel on Culture*, London: Sage, 1998, 187–205.

90. David Beer, *Popular Culture and New Media: The Politics of Circulation*, Basingstoke: Palgrave Macmillan, 2013.

91. *Bullseye* was a darts based TV game show. Hosted by Jim Bowen and broadcast on ITV, it originally ran from 1981 to 1995.

92. For a discussion of this see Graeme Turner, *Ordinary People and the Media: The Demotic Turn*, London: Sage, 2010.

93. Paul Long, Sarah Baker, Lauren Istvandity & Jez Collins, 'A labour of love: the affective archives of popular music culture', Archives and Records, 38(1), 2017, 61–79.

94. Mike Featherstone, 'Archive', *Theory, Culture & Society*, 23(2–3): 591–596, 2006.

95. Simon Reynolds, *Retromania: Pop Culture's Addiction to its Own Past*, London: Faber & Faber, 2012.

96. Paul Long, Sarah Baker, Lauren Istvandity, Jez Collins, 'A labour of love: the affective archives of popular music culture', *Archive and Records* 38(1), 2017, 61–79.

97. Andy Bennett, 'Punk's not dead: The continuing significance of punk rock for an older generation of fans', *Sociology* 40(2), 2006, 219–235.

98. Official Charts, 'The Top 40 best-selling cassettes of 2018', 7 January 2019, https://www.officialcharts.com/chart-news/ the-top-40-bestselling-cassettes-of-2018__25273/

99. This comeback was very widely publicised, see, for example, the announcement by Mark Savage at the BBC on the 24 April 2017 https://www.bbc.co.uk/news/entertainment-arts-39691240

100. See Damien Jones, 'Elastics reunite and return to the studio', *NME*, 23 January 2017, https://www.nme.com/news/music/elastica-reunite-return-studio-1956368

101. John Matson, 'Is pop music evolving? Or is it just getting louder', *Scientific American*, 26 July 2012, https://blogs.scientificamerican. com/observations/is-pop-music-evolving-or-is-it-just-getting-louder/

102. An article in the *Tornado Times*, which has since been removed, was titled 'Today's music lacks authenticity and creativity', http:// thetornadotimes.com/opinion/todays-music-lacks-authenticity-and-creativity-s/

103. An article in *PPCorn*, which has also since been removed, was titled 'The demise of creativity in the music industry', http://ppcorn.com/ us/2016/01/02/the-demise-of-creativity-in-the-music-industry/

104. Lee Barron, 'Back on record – The reasons behind vinyl's unlikely comeback', *The Conversation*, 17 April 2015, https://theconversation. com/back-on-record-the-reasons-behind-vinyls-unlikely-comeback-39964

105. Simon Reynolds, *Retromania: Pop Culture's Addiction to its Own Past*, London: Faber & Faber, 2012.

106. David Beer, 'Making friends with Jarvis Cocker: Music culture in the context of Web 2.0', *Cultural Sociology* 2(2), 222–241, 2008.

107. Andy Bennett, 'Punk's not dead: The continuing significance of punk rock for an older generation of fans', *Sociology* 40(2), 2006, 219–235.

108. See or instance Andy Bennett & Paul Hodkinson, *Ageing and Youth Cultures: Music, Style and Identity*, London: Berg, 2012.

109. On this point see also Paul Hodkinson, 'Ageing in a spectacular youth culture: Continuity, change and community in the Goth scene', *British Journal of Sociology* 62(2), 2011, 262–282.

110. Tia DeNora, *Music in Everyday Life*, Cambridge: Cambridge University Press, 2000.

111. Lee Barron, 'Back on record – The reasons behind vinyl's unlikely comeback', *The Conversation*, 17 April 2015, https://theconversation.com/back-on-record-the-reasons-behind-vinyls-unlikely-comeback-39964

112. Henry Irving, 'Keep calm and carry on conquered the world, but it was too mundane for World War II', *The Conversation*, 27 June 2014, https://theconversation.com/keep-calm-and-carry-on-conquered-the-world-but-it-was-too-mundane-for-world-war-ii-28519

113. See chapter 3 in David Beer, *Popular Culture and New Media: The Politics of Circulation*, Basingstoke: Palgrave Macmillan, 2013.

114. This was widely reported at the time, see, for example, Alex Hern, 'Snapchat Memories: the photo messaging service is less ephemeral than ever', *The Guardian*, 7 July 2016.

115. Mike Featherstone, 'Archive', *Theory, Culture & Society* 23(2–3), 2006, 591–596.

116. Amongst a wide range of coverage around privacy see, for example, Eerke Boiten, 'Investigatory powers bill will remove ISPs' right to protect your privacy', *The Conversation*, 5 November 2015, https://

theconversation.com/investigatory-powers-bill-will-remove-isps-right-to-protect-your-privacy-50178

117. Alyson Leigh Young & Anabel Quan-Haase, 'Privacy protection strategies on Facebook: The internet privacy paradox revisited', *Information, Communication & Society* 16(4), 2013, 479–500.

118. Mike Featherstone, 'Archive', *Theory, Culture & Society* 23(2–3), 2006, 591–596.

119. Jian Raymond Rui & Michael A. Stefanone, 'Strategic image management online: Self-presentation, self-esteem and social network perspectives', *Information, Communication, & Society* 16(8), 2013, 1286–1305.

120. For an early discussion of this in the context of social media see Zygmunt Bauman, *Consuming Life*, Cambridge: Polity Press, 2007.

121. See Jacques Derrida, *Archive Fever: A Freudian Impression*, Chicago: University of Chicago Press, 1998.

122. See Georg Simmel, 'Bridge & Door', *Theory, Culture & Society* 11(1), 1994, 5–10.

123. Sherry Turkle, *Evocative Objects: Things We Think With*, Massachusetts: MIT Press, 2011.

124. Sherry Turkle, p. 5.

125. Daniel Miller, *The Comfort of Things*, Cambridge: Polity Press, 2009.

126. See the essay 'Unpacking my library', in Walter Benjamin (ed.), *Illuminations*, New York: Pimlico, 1999.

127. Marshall McLuhan & Quentin Fiore, *The Medium is the Massage*, London: Penguin, 1967.

128. David Beer, 'Tune-out: Music, soundscapes and the urban Mise-en-scene', *Information, Communication & Society* 10(6), 846–866, 2007.

129. Sophie Arkette, 'Sounds like city', *Theory, Culture & Society* 21(1), 159–168, 2004.

130. Peter Sloterdijk, *Bubbles: Spheres Volume 1: Microspherology*, New York: Semiotext(e), 2011.

131. Philip Mirowski, *Never Let a Serious Crisis Go to Waste: How Neoliberalism Survived the Financial Meltdown*, London: Verso, 2014, p. 92.

132. Information about Smartwater can be found at https://www.drinksmartwater.com

133. The advert can be viewed at https://www.youtube.com/watch?v=fsFkwaI6lf0

134. Amongst many instances, see, for example, the smart home depicted in this video https://www.youtube.com/watch?v=f8giE7i7CAE

135. A further example of the smart home can be found described here https://www.technologyreview.com/s/523431/ces-2014-smart-homes-open-their-doors/

136. See Delphine Strauss, 'Mapping the economy in real time is almost in our grasp', *Financial Times*, 30 April 2018, https://www.ft.com/content/58190dc2-4c79-11e8-97e4-13afc22d86d4

137. See chapter 8 in Donna Haraway, *Simians, Cyborgs, and Women: The Reinvention of Nature*, London: Free Association Books, 1991.

138. James Harkin, 'Cyborg city', *The Guardian*, 26 November 2005, https://www.theguardian.com/technology/2005/nov/26/news.comment

139. Pierre Dardot & Christian Laval, *The New Way of the World: On Neoliberal Society*, London: Verso, 2014, p. 272.

140. Philip Mirowski, *Never Let a Serious Crisis Go to Waste: How Neoliberalism Survived the Financial Meltdown*, London: Verso, 2014.

141. William Davies, *Nervous States: How Feeling Took Over the World*, London: Jonathan Cape, 2018.

142. Eli Pariser neatly described and reflects on his concept in the TED2011 talk 'Beware online "filter bubbles"', available at https://www.ted.com/talks/eli_pariser_beware_online_filter_bubbles

143. Bartlett was writing about the pre-print version, the final article is: Brenden Nyhan & Jason Reifler, 'When corrections fail: The persistence of political misperceptions', *Political Behaviour* 32(2), 303–330.

144. Jamie Bartlett, 'Why the 'backfire effect' is damaging political debate', *Medium*, 15 July 2017, https://medium.com/@jamie.bartlett/why-the-backfire-effect-is-damaging-political-debate-fa13f6d7d3c3

145. Imogen Tyler & Bruce Bennett, 'Celebrity Chav: Fame, Femininity and Social Class', *European Journal of Cultural Studies* 13(3), 2010, 375–393.

146. See, for example, the audio podcast 'Who or what is Cambridge Analytica?', *Financial Times*, 22 March 2018, https://www.ft.com/video/517a016d-642e-4a67-94f5-214dffd96a14

147. Hannah Summers & Nicola Slawson, 'Investigators complete seven-hour Cambridge Analytica HQ search', *The Guardian*, 24 March 2018, https://www.theguardian.com/news/2018/mar/23/judge-grants-search-warrant-for-cambridge-analyticas-offices

148. Channel 4 news documentary '*Exposed: Undercover secrets of Trump's data firm*', available on All 4 at https://www.channel4.com/news/exposed-undercover-secrets-of-donald-trump-data-firm-cambridge-analytica

149. David Beer, 'Cambridge Analytica: the data analytics industry is already in full swing', *The Conversation*, 23 March 2018, https://theconversation.com/cambridge-analytica-the-data-analytics-industry-is-already-in-full-swing-93873

150. Michael Wade, 'Psychographics: the behavioural analytics that helped Cambridge Analytica know voter's minds', *The Conversation*, 21 March 2018, https://theconversation.com/psychographics-the-behavioural-analysis-that-helped-cambridge-analytica-know-voters-minds-93675

151. David Beer, 'Data-led politics: do analytics have the power that we are led to believe?', LSE British Politics & Policy, 3 March 2017, http://blogs.lse.ac.uk/politicsandpolicy/the-politics-of-data-led-campaigning/

152. Nick Srnicek, *Platform Capitalism*, Cambridge: Polity Press, 2016.

153. Vivienne Tay, 'Facebook loses US$60bn in market value following user data scandal', *Marketing*, 21 March 2018, http://www.marketing-interactive.com/facebook-loses-us60bn-in-market-value-following-user-data-scandal/

154. Tiziana Terranova, 'Free labor: Producing culture for the digital economy', *Social Text* 18(2), 2000, 33–58.

155. See, for example, Matthew Lawrence & Laurie Laybourn-Langton, 'The digital commonwealth: From private enclosure to collective benefit', IPPR, 7 September 2018, https://www.ippr.org/research/publications/the-digital-commonwealth

156. Tom Mills, 'We need a nationalised alternative to Facebook – And the BBC could provide the answer', *Independent*, 22 March 2018, https://www.independent.co.uk/voices/facebook-cambridge-analytica-bbc-nationalised-alternative-a8269066.html

157. Paul Mason, 'Choice: Break up Facebook – Or take it into public ownership?' Novara, 19 March 2018, https://novaramedia.com/2018/03/19/choice-break-up-facebook-or-take-it-into-public-ownership-i-am-not-kidding/

158. Robert Reich, 'Break up Facebook (and while we're at it, Google, Apple and Amazon)', *The Guardian*, 20 November 2018, https://www.theguardian.com/commentisfree/2018/nov/20/facebook-google-antitrust-laws-gilded-age

159. Kadhim Shubber, 'Facebook poaches antitrust enforcer from DoJ', *Financial Times*, 21 November 2018.

160. Guy Standing, 'Why you've never heard of a Charter that's as important as the Magna Carta', *Open Democracy*, 6 November 2017, https://www.opendemocracy.net/uk/guy-standing/why-youve-never-heard-of-charter-thats-as-important-as-magna-carta

161. The video of the hearing 'Facebook, social media privacy, and the use and abuse of data', 10 April 2018, can be viewed at https://www.judiciary.senate.gov/meetings/facebook-social-media-privacy-and-the-use-and-abuse-of-data

162. The statement from Facebook can be found at https://docs.house.gov/meetings/IF/IF00/20180411/108090/HHRG-115-IF00-Wstate-ZuckerbergM-20180411.pdf

163. See for instance David Lyon, *Surveillance Society: Monitoring everyday life*, Milton-Keynes: Open University Press, 2001.

164. The press release concerning this initiative was available at http://www.channel4.com/info/press/news/channel-4-launches-worlds-first-audio-personalised-tv-ads

165. As described at http://www.channel4.com/info/press/news/channel-4-launches-worlds-first-audio-personalised-tv-ads

166. Louis Althusser, *On the Reproduction of Capitalism*, London: Verso, 2014.

167. Eva Illouz, *Cold Intimacies: The Making of Emotional Capitalism*, Cambridge: Polity Press, 2007.

168. William Davies, 'The Mismanaged Heart', *Real Life*, 3 August 2016, https://reallifemag.com/the-mismanaged-heart/

169. Mark Andrejevic, *Infoglut: How too much information is changing the way we think and know*, London: Routledge, 2013.

170. Such references are usually fleeting and evoke the adaptation of Jeremey Bentham's ideas provided by Michel Foucault in his classic book *Discipline and Punish*, London: Penguin, 1991.

171. Dylan Curran, 'Are your phone camera and microphone spying on you?', *The Guardian*, 6 April 2018, https://www.theguardian.com/commentisfree/2018/apr/06/phone-camera-microphone-spying

172. Andrew Griffin, 'Facebook is using smartphones to Listen to what people say, Professor suggests', *Independent*, 31 May 2016, https://www.independent.co.uk/life-style/gadgets-and-tech/news/facebook-using-people-s-phones-to-listen-in-on-what-they-re-saying-claims-professor-a7057526.html?amp

173. Adam Sherwin, 'New BBC iPlayer will know who is on your sofa', *i newspaper*, 3 August 2017.

174. Alex Hern, 'UK homes vulnerable to 'staggering' levels of corporate surveillance', *The Guardian*, 1 June 2018, https://www.theguardian.com/technology/2018/jun/01/uk-homes-vulnerable-to-staggering-level-of-corporate-surveillance

175. For a brief discussion of this episode see Chris Harnick's review, *EOnline*, 26 March 2017, https://www.eonline.com/news/838568/

the-good-fight-pits-matthew-perry-and-carrie-preston-against-each-
other-for-a-final-time-this-season

176. Christopher Mele, 'Bid for access to Amazon Echo audio in murder
     case raises privacy concerns', *The New York Times*, 28 December
     2016, https://www.nytimes.com/2016/12/28/business/amazon-echo-
     murder-case-arkansas.html

177. For an example of this see Rhiannon Williams, 'Alexa recorded
     couple's chat and sent it to a friend', *i newspaper*, 26 May 2018.

178. BBC News, 'Amazon Patents 'voice-sniffing' algorithms', *BBC*, 11
     April 2018, https://www.bbc.co.uk/news/technology-43725708

179. Olivia Solon, 'Facebook patents system that can use your
     phone's mic to monitor TV habits', *The Guardian*, 29 June
     2018, https://www.theguardian.com/technology/2018/jun/28/
     facebook-patent-phone-mic-listening-tv-shows

180. Chris Weller, 'Employees at a dozen Fortune 500 companies
     wear digital badges that watch and listen to their every move',
     Business Insider, 20 October 2016, http://uk.businessinsider.com/
     humanyze-badges-watch-and-listen-employees-2016-10

181. Scott Carey, 'US biometrics startup Humanyze is bringing its
     employee tracking badges to the UK', *Techworld*, 26 January 2017,
     https://www.techworld.com/startups/us-startup-humanyze-is-
     bringing-its-employee-tracking-badges-uk-3653590/

182. See, for example, Phoebe Moore, *The Quantified Self in Precarity:
     Work, Technology and What Counts*, London: Routledge, 2017.

183. Martin Dodge & Rob Kitchin, 'Software, objects and home space',
     Environment and Planning A: Economy and Space 41(6), 1344–1365,
     2009.

184. Phoebe Moore, *The Quantified Self in Precarity: Work, Technology
     and What Counts*, London: Routledge, 2017.

185. It was the *New Statesman* magazine dated 29 June 2018.

186. Richard Waters, 'Facebook rushes to resolve data-sharing problems
     and regain user trust', *Financial Times*, 19 December 2018.

187. See for instance, Mark Sweeney 'Young adults swapping Facebook for Snapchat', *The Guardian*, 28 August 2018.

188. Pew Research Centre, 'Teens, social media & technology 2018', Pew, 31 May 2018, available at http://www.pewinternet.org/2018/05/31/teens-social-media-technology-2018/

189. The same Pew Research Centre report on 'Teens, social media & technology 2018' also claimed that 45% percent of the respondents claimed they were online almost constantly.

190. Georg Simmel, 'The crisis of culture', in Peter A. Lawrence (ed.) and D.E. Jenkinson (trans.), *Georg Simmel: Sociologist and European*, New York: Barnes & Noble, 1976, pp. 253–266.

191. David Frisby, *Fragments of Modernity*, Cambridge: Polity Press, 1985, p. 39.

192. Discussed in David Beer, *Georg Simmel's Concluding Thoughts: Worlds, Lives, Fragments*, London: Palgrave Macmillan, 2019.

193. Jamie Bartlett, 'The war between technology and democracy', *Medium*, 18 September 2018, https://medium.com/@jamie.bartlett/the-war-between-technology-democracy-5ca57292956a

194. See Georg Simmel, *The View of Life: Four Metaphysical Essays with Journal Aphorisms*, Chicago: University of Chicago Press, 2010, p. 55.

195. Nick Srnicek, *Platform Capitalism*, Cambridge: Polity Press, 2017. p. 129.

196. Nick Srnicek, p. 7.

197. Jeremy Rifkin, *The Age of Access: How the Shift from Ownership to Access Is Transforming Modern Life*, London: Penguin, 2001.

198. David Frisby, *Sociological Impressionism: A Reassessment of Georg Simmel's Social Theory*, Second Edition, London: Routledge, 1992.

199. For a discussion of this see Carl Miller, *The Death of the Gods: The New Global Power Grab*, London: William Heinemann, 2018.

INDEX